DICTIONARY OF
BOTANY AND PALEOBOTANY

DICTIONARY
OF
BOTANY AND PALEOBOTANY

Edited by
Er. Haojam Rocky Singh
Richa Chowdhary

***JNANADA PRAKASHAN* (P&D)**
in association with
THE GLOBAL OPEN UNIVERSITY
NAGALAND (INDIA)

Published by :
JNANADA PRAKASHAN (P&D)
4837/2, 24, Ansari Road, Daryaganj
New Delhi-110002
Phone : 011-23272047
Mobile : 9212137080
Email: jnanadabooksdelhi@yahoo.com
Website: www.jnanadabooks.com; text.ind.in

Assisted by :
TEXT BOOK PROMOTION SOCIETY OF INDIA
4837/2, 24, Ansari Road, Daryaganj
New Delhi-110002
Phone : 011-23272047
Mobile : 9212137080

Edition: 2016

Dictionary of Botany and Paleobotany
ISBN: 978-81-7139-453-1

Typesetting by :
Vardhman Computers
New Delhi-110017

Published by Mrs. S. Chowdhary for M/s. Jnanada Prakashan (P&D) Daryaganj, Ansari Road, New Delhi-110 002 and *printed at* Balaji Offset, Navin Shahdara, Delhi-110032.

Plants are the basis of our existence and prosperity. We get fod, medicine, paper, wood-made furniture etc. from plants. In this sense, the study of botany is very useful to all human beings. This is the age of science and scientific revolutions Every now and then, we hear of amazing scientific inventions that are adding to the comforts of man. Albeit, many books are available in market on botany and paleobotany subject, but as far as the dictionary on this subject is concerned, it can be counted on fingers. Moreover, foreign author dictionaries are beyond the mental horizon of Indian students.

Keeping all these factors in mind, the editor of this dictionary has done marathon research work while compiling the dictionary of Botany and Paleobotany. Extra care has been taken so that latest scientific word should be included in the dictionary.

The scope of biology and its branches are spreading like never before. Indian students are making their presence felt in foreign universities and are passing out with flying colours. The green revolution was a dramatic increase in agricultural yields that occurred in the 1950s through 1960s. The green revolution was based on many scientific improvements in plant science, including the genetic improvements of many plants, improved irrigation, more efficient machinery, new fertilizers, and pest-controls. It increased plants disease-resistance, improved their hardiness, and increased their productivity especially of rice, wheat and corn.

Biology is a general term used in a very broad field of study. In all its manifestations, biology is one of the major scientific areas of public interest at the beginning of second decade of new millennium.

Considering the need of botany students of higher studies, this dictionary has been carefully prepared in response to their needs. There are one thousand and seven hundred entries in this dictionary. Students appearing for competitive examinations like IFS (Indian Forest Service), IAS, CPMT etc will find this dictionary very helpful and handy.

Suggestions are welcome for improving the next edition of this important publication.

ABAXIAL

Abaxial means being located on the side away from the axis. The abaxial surface of a leaf is its underside.

ABSCISIC ACID

Abscisic acid is a plant hormone that inhibits growth, causes the abscission of leaves, induces dormancy, closes stomata, and triggers other phenomena in response to adverse conditions.

ABSCISSION

Abscission is the normal separation of a leaf, fruit, or flower from a plant. Abscisic acid is the plant hormone involved in abscission.

ABSCISSION ZONE

The abscission zone is the area at the base of leaf's petiole, a fruit stalk, or a branch in which the separation (abscission) layer develops. The disintegration of this layer causes a leaf, fruit, or flower to fall from a plant. Abscisic acid is the plant hormone involved in this process.

ACICULAR

Acicular means needle-like. For example, pine needles are acicular.

ACID RAIN

Acid rain is polluted and harmful to the environment. Acid rain has a low pH. Acid rain may have been a component of the K-T extinction.

ACHENE

An achene is a dry, indehiscent one-seeded fruit with a leathery pericarp that is easily separated from the seed coat. For example, sunflower.

ADAPTIVE RADIATION

Adaptive radiation is the diversification of a species as it adapts to different ecological niches. If successful, the species becomes specialized for the new environments, and they eventually evolve into different species.

ADAXIAL

Adaxial means being located on the side towards the axis. The adaxial surface of a leaf is the upper side.

ADENOSINE TRIPHOSPHATE

ATP (short for adenosine triphosphate) is a nucleotide that has a ribose sugar and three phosphate groups. ATP is a high-energy molecule used for energy storage by organisms. In plant cells, ATP is produced in the cristae of mitochondria and chloroplasts.

ADVENTITIOUS

Adventitious organs are those organs that grow from an unusual part of the plant. For example, fibrous adventitious roots grow from the trunk above the ground instead of starting underground.

AERIAL ROOT

An aerial root is a plant's root that is produced above the ground.

AGE

An age is a unit of geological time which is distinguished by some feature (like an Ice Age). An age is shorter than epoch, usually lasting from a few millions of years to about a hundred million years.

AGRICULTURE

Agriculture is the science of farming, including growing plants and raising animals.

AGROFORESTRY

Agroforestry is a land use system in which woody perennials are grown with agricultural crops (together with other land uses, like animal production).

AGROLOGY

Agrology is a branch of soil science that studies the soil used in producing crops.

AGROSTOLOGY

Agrostology is a branch of botany that studies grasses.

AIR SPACE

Air space is the intercellular gaps within the spongy mesophyll of leaves. These gaps are filled with gas that the plant uses (carbon dioxide - CO_2) and gases that the plant is expelling (oxygen - O_2, and water vapor).

AIR PLANT

Air plants (also called epiphytes) are plants that live attached to a plant (or other structure like a telephone pole or a building) and not in the ground). Epiphytes include many orchids and bromeliads. Epiphytes are not parasites; they get water and nutrients from the air (and not from their host).

ALGAE

Algae are simple photosynthetic organisms that belong to the kingdom Protista. Most algae are aquatic; seaweeds are algae. Some algae are unicellular while others are multicellular.

ALIEN

An alien is a plant that is not native to a place; it came from another place.

ALOE

Aloes are succulent, clumping plants with fleshy, toothed (non-fibrous) leaves. There are about 300 species of aloe; they live in warm, dry habitats and most originated in northern Africa. Aloe vera is a popular plant whose gel-like sap is used as a medicinal salve; it is originally from northern Africa, the Cape Verde Islands, and the Canary Islands. Aloe vera has gray-green leaves and tubular yellow flowers that grow on a stalk that is up to 3 feet tall. Classification: Family Liliceae (lilies). Genua Aloe, Species - about 300 including *A. vera, A. ferox,* etc.

ALTERNATE

An alternate pattern of leaves or buds is a pattern in which there is one leaf (or bud) per node, and on the opposite side of the stem (not in pairs).

ALVAREZ THEORY OF EXTINCTION

This theory is that a large asteroid, meteor, or comet hit the earth 65 million years ago, causing huge atmospheric and geologic disruptions, leading to a mass extinction which killed the dinosaurs and many other plant and animal species.

AMBER

Amber is a yellowish, fossilized tree resin (from conifers) that sometimes contains bits of trapped matter.

AMYLOPLAST

A organelle (with double membranes) in some plant cells that stores starch. Amyloplasts are found in starchy plants like tubers and fruitsr.

ANGIOSPERM

Angiosperms, meaning "covered seed" are flowering plants. They produce seeds enclosed in fruit (an ovary). They are the dominant type of plant today; there are over 250,000 species. Their flowers are used in reproduction. Angiosperms evolved about 145 million years ago, during the late Jurassic period, and were eaten by dinosaurs. They became the dominant land plants about 100 million years ago (edging out conifers, a type of gymnosperm). Angiosperms are divided into the monocots (like corn) and dicots (like beans).

ANNUAL

An annual is a plant that goes through its entire life cycle within a year. It grows from a seed, matures, produces seed, and dies within a year.

ANNUAL RING

Annual rings are concentric circles that appear on tree trunk cross-sections that mark the end of a growing season. These rings show whether the tree grew a lot or a little that year.

ANTHER

The anther is the tip of a flower's stamen. The anther contains the pollen

ANTHOPHYTA

Anthophyta are flowering plants, the largest group of plants (which includes the grasses). The flowers are used in reproduction. They evolved during the Cretaceous period.

APICAL DOMINANCE

Apical dominance is the phenomenon in which a terminal (end) bud inhibits the development of lateral (side) buds.

APICAL MERISTEM

The apical meristem consists of meristematic cells located at the tip (apex) of a root or shoot.

APOGEOTROPIC ROOTS

Apogeotropic roots are roots that grow upwards to the soil surface (other roots grow downwards), emerging from the soil and growing upwards. The sego palm has apogeotropic roots, as do cycads.

APOMIXIS

Apomixis is a type of reproduction in which a plant produces seeds without fertilization.

APOMORPHY

An apomorphy is a new genetic characteristic common to a clade. Feathers are an apomorphy for birds.

APPLESEED, JOHNNY

Johnny Appleseed was a man who spread apple trees through the USA. His real name was John Chapman, but he was called Johnny Appleseed because of his love for growing apple trees.

AQUATIC

Aquatic organisms are those found in water. Many plants are aquatic, including seaweeds.

ARABLE

Arable land is suitable for growing crop plants.

ARBOREAL

Arboreal means living in trees. Many animals are arboreal, including the sugar glider.

ARBORETUM

An arboretum is a park or garden where trees and shrubs are grown for educational and/or scientific uses.

ARCUATE

Leaves with arcuate venation have veins that are curve towards the apex (tip).

AREOLE

Areoles are circular clusters of spines on a cactus. Flowers bud at an areole and new stems branch from an areole.

ARID

An arid area is dry and hot, with little rainfall and few plants.

ASTEROID

An asteroid is a large rock or small planet orbiting the Sun. Most asteroids lie in a belt between Mars and Jupiter. An asteroid impact with the earth may have caused the K-T mass extinction.

ATMOSPHERE

The atmosphere is the mixture of gases that surrounds the earth. The earth's atmosphere is mostly nitrogen.

ATOM

Everything is made up of tiny atoms. An atom is the smallest part of an element that has the properties of that element.

AUTOTROPH

An autotroph (or producer) is an organism that makes its own food from light energy or chemical energy without eating. Most green plants, many protists (one-celled organisms like slime molds) and most bacteria are autotrophs. Autotrophs are the base of the food chain.

AUXIN

Auxins are growth hormones found in plants. Auxins induce phototropism, apical dominance, cell elongation and many other reactions.

AWN

The awn is a bristle-like extension of a plant near its tip.

AXIL

The axil of a plant is the angle between the upper side of the stem and a leaf, branch, or petiole. In flowering plants, the bud develops in the axil of a leaf.

AXILLARY BUD

The axillary bud is a bud that develops in the axil (the angle between the stem and the leaf) of a plant.

AXIS

The axis of a plant runs through the middle of it, e.g., the stem of a plant or the rachis of a compound leaf.

B

BACKGROUND EXTINCTIONS

Background extinctions are those extinctions that occur continuously throughout time. These extinctions are caused by small changes in climate or habitat, depleted resources, competition, and other changes that require adaptation and flexibility. Most extinctions (perhaps up to 95 per cent of all extinctions) occur as background extinctions.

BACTERIUM

A bacterium (plural bacteria) is a microscopic, prokaryotic, single-celled organism with a cell wall. Bacteria reproduce by binary fission. Bacteria are one ot the earliest forms of life. Some bacteria (rhizobia) are nitrogen-fixing; they transform nitrogen gas in the atmopshere into a form that can be used by plants.

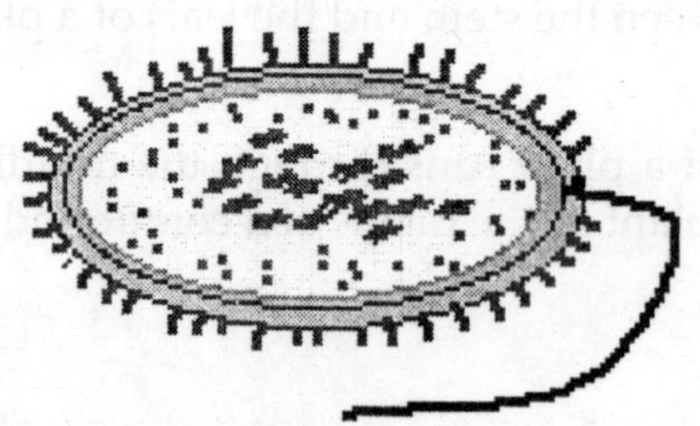

BADLANDS

Badlands are barren, severely eroded places on the earth where the soft rock layers are sculpted into beautiful forms. These exposed rock layers are often wonderful places in which to find fossils. They're called badlands because the land is useless for farming and many other human purposes.

BAMBOO

Bamboo is a fast-growing monocot grass.

BANANA

The banana tree is an herbaceous plant (because there is no woody tissue in the stem), it is also considered a fruit (because the seeds of the plant are contained within the banana).

BARK

The bark is the outer covering of the trunk, branches, and roots of trees.

BARLEY

Barley is a cereal grain related to wheat, oats, and rice. Barley seeds (the part of the plant that is highest in nutrition) grow in spikes at the tips of the stems - it resembles wheat. This important crop is grown in temperate areas and is used as animal feed, for malt (used in making beer, malted milk, and food flavoring), and for human consumption (used as a flour, a thickener, a cereal, in soups, etc.). Barley was cultivated thousands of years ago; it was grown by the Egyptians from 5,000 to 7,000 years ago. The countries that produce the most barley are Russia, Canada, and Germany. Classification: family Poaceae (Gramineae) (grasses), genus Hordeum, species H. vulgare.

BENNETTITALEANS

Bennettitaleans, also called cycadeoids, are primitive plants (gymnosperms) that resemble cycads (but they are not cycads), but have different methods of reproduction. Bennettitaleans lived throughout the Mesozoic era. Examples of bennettitaleans include Williamsonia (Jurassic through end Cretaceous), Williamsoniella (Jurassic through end Cretaceous), and Zamites (Triassic).

BERRY

A berry is a small, juicy, fleshy, stoneless fruit that contains one or many seeds. This simple fruit has a pulpy pericarp surrounding the seed. Some berries include the gooseberry, tomato, currant, and grape.

BIENNIAL

Biennial means that it takes two years to complete the full life cycle.

BILATERAL

Bilateral means two sides.

BILLION

A billion is a thousand million. Multicellular life evolved on the earth about a billion years ago.

BINOMIAL NOMENCLATURE

Binomial nomenclature is a system developed by Linnaeus for giving organisms scientific names in which each organism has a genus name (always capitalized) and a species name (not capitalized). For example, the Venus flytrap is *Dionaea muscipula,* and people are *Homo sapiens*.

BIODIVERSITY

Biodiversity is the abundance of different plant and animal species found in an environment.

BIOLOGICAL MAGNIFICATION

Biological magnification is the phenomenon in which toxins (poisons) are more and more concentrated in living organisms that are higher up in trophic levels of the food web. For example, if a small amount of toxins is in plants, the animal that eat those plants have a higher concentration of the toxins, and the meat-eaters that eat those plant-eaters have even higher levels of the toxin. The toxins are from pesticides (bug killing chemicals), herbicides (weed-killing chemicals) and waste materials.

BIOMASS

A biomass is the total amount of living material in an area. It is calculated by adding up the weights of all of the organisms.

BIRCH

Birch (genus Betula, many species) are broad-leafed, deciduous trees and shrubs with paper-like bark.

BLADDER

A bladder is a small, air filled sac. Some plants, like bladderwort (a seaweed), have air bladders.

BLADE

A blade is a narrow, flat leaf.

BLUE-GREEN ALGAE

Blue-green algae (also called cyanobacteria) are simple, (usually) one-celled photosynthetic organisms that lack a membrane-bound nucleus (they are prokaryotic). They have a primitive, bacteria-like cell structure (lacking a nucleus and other organelles); although they ahve photosynthetic pigments, they lack chloroplasts (the specialized photosynthetic organelles seen in higher plants). Blue-green algae belong to the kingdom Monera.

BOLIDE

A bolide is a meteor, asteroid, or comet that hits the earth and explodes.

BOTANIST

A botanist is a scientist who studies plants.

BOTANY

Botany is the scientific study of plants.

BRACT

A bract is a reduced, leaf-like structure that is associated with a flower or a cone.

BRANCH

A branch is a part of a tree or shrub that grows from the trunk or stem.

BROMELIAD

Bromeliads are a group of plants that have stiff, waxy leaves that form a cup-shaped body. This "cup" catches and retains water during wet weather, and the plant uses this water to live through dry spells. Most bromeliads are xerophytes (able to tolerate a dry environment) and epiphytes (living attached to another plant and not rooted in the ground). Classification: Division Magnoliophyta (Angioperms), Class Liliopsida (monocots), Subclass Zingiberidae, Order Bromeliales, Family Bromeliaceae (Bromeliads). Bromeliads were named for the Swedish botanist Olaus Bromelius (1639-1705).

BROWSER

A browser is an animal that eats tall foliage (leaves). Many sauropod dinosaurs, like Brachiosaurus and Ultrasauros, were browsers.

BRYOPHYTES

Bryophytes (Phylum Bryophta) include the hornworts (Class Anthocerotae), liverworts (Class Hepaticae), and mosses (Class Musci). These low-growing plants do not have true roots, leaves, or stems - they also lack a vascular system (the internal tubes that transport food and water in more advanced plants). Bryophytes probably evolved from green algae; fossils of bryophytes are rare.

BUD

A bud is a small, developing part of a plant that will grow into a flower, a new leaf or a stem.

BUD SCALE

A bud scale is a modified leaf (or similar structure) that covers and protects the bud.

BULB

A bulb is an underground stem, usually globular, that has fleshy leaves emerging from the top and roots emerging from the bottom. The fleshy leaves store food. Examples include the tulip, narcissus, and onion.

BULBEL

A bulbel (also called a bulbet) is a small bulb that grows from another bulb. This is an example of vegetative proagation.

BURBANK, LUTHER

Luther Burbank (1849-1926) was an American plant breeder who developed over 800 new strains of plants, including many popular varieties of potato, plums, prunes, berries, trees, and flowers. One of his greatest inventions was the Russet Burbank potato (also called the Idaho potato), which he developed in 1871. This blight-resistant potato helped Ireland recover from its devastating potato famine of 1840-60. Burbank also developed the Flaming Gold nectarine, the Santa Rosa plum, and the Shasta daisy. Burbank was raised on a farm and only went to elementary school; he was self-educated. Burbank applied the works of Charles Darwin to plants. Of Darwin's *The Variation of Animals and Plants under Domestication*, Burbank said, "It opened up a new world to me."

BURGESS SHALE

The burgess shale is an incredibly fossil-rich area in the Canadian Rocky Mountains (in British Columbia). This Lagerstatten (a geological fossil deposit rich with varied, well-preserved fossils) is replete with fossils from the Cambrian Period, roughly 500 million years old. The Burgess shale was discovered in 1909 by Charles Doolittle Wolcott, who was the Secretary of the Smithsonian Institution in Washington, D.C. at the time. Fossils from this area include early representatives of most modern groups, including plants, worms, sponges, shrimp-like crustaceans, and jellyfish.

BUTTRESSES

Buttresses are tree trunk supports that help hold up tall trees in rainforests. They are needed to stabilize the tree because the soil is shallow (only a few inches deep) and the tree roots do not penetrate very deeply into the earth.

C

C3 PLANT

A C3 plant is one that produces phosphoglyceric acid, (a molecule that has three carbon atoms) as a stable intermediary in the first step in photosynthesis (the Calvin Cycle). Most plants on the earth (over 95 percent) are C3 plants.

C4 PLANT

A C4 plant is one that produces oxaloacetic acid (a molecule that has four carbon atoms) as a stable intermediary in the first step in photosynthesis. Very few plants on the earth (less than 1 percent) are C4 plants (including corn and sugarcane). Photorespiration in C4 plants is more efficient in strong light. The processes in C4 biochemistry were studied by M. D. Hatch and C. R. Slack.

CACAO

The cacao plant (*Theobroma cacao*) is a evergreen flowering tree native to wet, warm forests of South and Central America. This tree grows to 40 feet (12 m) tall. After flowering, 10 to 14-inch long red fruit pods develop. In each pod are almond-shaped cacao beans and pulp. Chocolate is made from the beans in the pods of the cacao plant.

CACTUS

A cactus (the plural is cacti) is a succulent plant that can live in dry areas. It has a structure that minimizes water loss. The stems are photosynthetic, green, and fleshy. The leaves are reduced to spines or are absent. Classification: Division Magnoliophyta (angioperms), Class Magnoliopsida (dicots), Subclass Caryophyllidae, Order Caryophyllales, Family Cactaceae (Cactus).

CALIFORNIA POPPY

A golden poppy (*Eschscholzia californica*) from western North America. It has finely-divided foliage and cup-shaped flowers.

CALVIN CYCLE

The second stage in the process of phtosynthesis is called the Calvin Cycle (it is also called the Calvin-Benson Cycle or the Carbon Fixation Cycle. In the Calvin Cycle, carbon molecules from carbon dioxide, CO_2, are fixed into the sugar glucose, ($C_6H_{12}O_2$) (in six repeats of the cycle). The Calvin Cycle takes place in the stroma of eucaryotic chloroplasts. The major enzyme that mediates the Calvin Cycle is Rubisco (ribulose-1-5-biphosphate carboxylase). The Calvin Cycle was first investigated in the late 1940s and early 1950s by the Nobel Prize winning chemist Melvin Calvin (1911-1997).

CALYX

The calyx is the sepals of a flower.

CAMBIUM

Cambium is a layer of dividing cells found in the stems of plants. The cambium forms the specialized xylem and phloem cells and causes the stem to increase in thickness.

CANOPY

The canopy consists of the upper parts of the trees of a rainforest (about 65 to 130 feet or 20 to 40 m above the ground). The canopy is the part of a forest in which the branches of the trees spread out and block sunlight from reaching the forest floor. This leafy environment is full of life in a tropical rainforest and includes insects, birds, reptiles, mammals, and more.

CAPILLARY ACTION

Capillary action is the movement of water as it is pulled upwards through tubes (xylem) within a plant's roots, stems, and leaves. The water (containing minerals and dissolved nutrients) is driven against gravity by adhesion of the water molecules (they stick to the sides of the tubes), cohesion of those molecules (the water molecules sticking together), and surface tension (the forces of the molecules on surface of the upward-moving water).

CAPSULE

A capsule is a seed pod that opens when it is dry and the seeds are mature.

CARBON DIOXIDE

Carbon dioxide, CO_2, is a molecule that has one carbon atom and two oxygen atoms; it is a gas at standard temperature and pressure. Plants use carbon dioxide gas in the photosynthetic process.

CARNIVORE

Carnivores are animals that eat meat. They usually have sharp teeth and powerful jaws.

CARPEL

The carpel is the female reproductive organ of a flower - it makes the seeds. It consists of the stigma, style and ovary. There may be more than one carpel in a flower.

CASPARIAN STRIP

The Casparian strip is waxy layer (a band of suberin, a waterproofing material) that is located in the walls of plant root cells. This barrier strip stops the transport of water and minerals into the main vascular system of the root.

CAUDEX

The caudex is an enlarged, woody base of the stem or trunk (located just below the gound) on some plants - it is used for water storage. Many desert plants have a caudex, an adaptation to dry conditions. Some palms, cycads, and succulents have a caudex.

CAUDICIFORM

Caudiciform means having a caudex.

CEDAR

Cedar trees (genus Cedrus) are large evergreen coniferous trees (up to about 80 feet tall) that have dense clusters of needles held in wide, woody peg-like structures. The barrel-shaped cones are held upright above a branch. Some cedars include: Cedar of Lebanon (*Cedrus libani*); Atlas cedar (*Cedrus atlantica*) - with blue-green foliage; Deodar cedar (*Cedrus deodara*) - with drooping branches.

CELL

The cell is the basic structural unit of all organisms. Plant cells have a tough outer cell wall, a cell membrane, genetic material (DNA), cytoplasm, and many organelles.

CELL MEMBRANE

A cell membrane (also called the plasma membrane or plasmalemma) surrounds each plant cell (it is located within the cell wall).

CELL WALL

Plant cells have a thick, rigid cell wall located outside the cell membrane. The cell wall is made of cellulose (a polysaccharide carbohydrate), proteins, and sometimes lignin. The cell wall gives the cell most of its support and structure. The cell wall also bonds with other cell walls to form the structure of the plant.

CELLULAR RESPIRATION

Cellular respiration is a process in which energy is produced from various molecules (like glucose), producing ATP (adenosine triphosphate). During cellular respiration, oxygen is used and carbon dioxide is produced Cellular respiration occurs in the mitochondria of eukaryotes, and in the cytoplasm of prokaryotes.

CELLULOSE

Cellulose is a carbohydrate that comprises much of a plant's cell, especially the cell wall.

CENOZOIC ERA

The "Age of Mammals" (65 million years ago to today), saw the emergence of familiar life forms, humans, the modern look of the continents, and a cooling climate. The Cenozoic (meaning "recent life") followed the Mesozoic era.

CENTROSOME

A centrosome (also called the "microtubule organizing center") is a small body located near the nucleus - it has a dense center and radiating tubules. The centrosome is where microtubules are made. During cell division (mitosis), the centrosome divides and the two parts move to opposite sides of the dividing cell.

CEREAL

A cereal is a grain that is used for human food. Some cereals include rice, oats, wheat, and barley.

CERRADO

The cerrado is a grassy, treeless plain that surrounds the Brazilian rainforest.

CHALK

Chalk is a soft, white type of limestone (a sedimentary rock). It consists mostly of calcium carbonate ($CaCO_3$) from ancient, microscopic, single-celled marine invertebrate shells. This type of rock is very porous, soft (a hardness of 3 on the Mohs scale), and crumbly. The chalk used to draw with is actually gypsum (calcium sulfate, $CaSO_4$-$2H_2O$)

CHARACTER

A character is a inherited trait of an organism. Characters are usually described in terms of a state, for example: "blue eyes" vs. "brown eyes," where "eyes" is the character, and "blue" and "brown" are its states.

CHICXULUB CRATER

The Chicxulub crater at the tip of the Yucatán Peninsula is an impact crater that dates from 65 million years ago. It is

120 miles wide and 1 mile deep. It is probably the site of the K-T meteorite impact that caused the extinction of the dinosaurs and many other groups of organisms.

CHLOROPHYLL

Chlorophyll is a molecule that can use light energy from sunlight to turn water and carbon dioxide gas into sugar and oxygen (this process is called photosynthesis). Chlorophyll is magnesium based and is usually green.

CHLOROPLAST

Chloroplasts are small green structures in plants that contain chlorophyll. Leaves have many chloroplasts.

CHONDRITIC METEOR

Chondritic meteors are stony meteors with chondrules, tiny glass spheres. These meteors are unchanged since their formation, shortly after the formation of the sun. These meteors consist of elements also common in the earth's core.

CHROMOSOME

Chromosomes are microscopic, self-replicating structures found in the nucleus of cells. Chromosomes contain genetic material (coiled stands of DNA that contain many genes). The genome of an organism is made up of the set of chromosomes that contain all of its genes. Chromosomes were discovered by Walther Fleming in 1879; the term chromosome was proposed by Waldeyer in 1888.

CINCHONA TREE

The cinchona tree is a tropical tree that is the primary source of the anit-malarial drug quinine. Quinine is found in the bark of the cinchona tree. Quinine is a chemical that cures malaria, a deadly tropical disease carried by mosquitoes. There are many species of cinchona; they range from about 15 to 20 meters tall. The cinchona tree is native to rainforests of the eastern slope of the Amazonian Andes of South America, where it is called the "fever tree." Classification: Family Rubiaceae, Genus Cinchona, Species C. officinalis, C. ledgeriana, C. uccirubra, C. calisaya, and others.

CLADODE

A cladode is a stem that looks like a leaf.

CLADE

A clade is a group of all the organisms that share a particular common ancestor (and therefore have similar features). The members of a clade are related to each other. A clade is monophyletic.

CLADISTICS

Cladistics is a method of classifying organisms based on common ancestry and the branching of the evolutionary family tree. Organisms that share common ancestors (and therefore have similar features) are grouped into taxonomic groups called clades. Cladistics can also be used to predict properties of yet-to-be discovered organisms.

CLADOGRAM

Cladograms are branching diagrams that depict species divergence from common ancestors. They show the distribution and origins of shared characteristics. Cladograms are testable hypotheses of phylogenetic relationships.

CLASS

In classification (taxonomy), a class is a group of related or similar organisms. A class contains one or more orders. A group of similar classes forms a phylum.

CLASSIFICATION

The classification of organisms helps in their study. Cladistics is a method based on common ancestry; the Linnean system is based on a simple hierarchical structure.

CLEFT

A cleft (also called parted) leaf is one in which the margins between the irregular teeth go more than halfway to the midrib.

CLOUD FOREST

A cloud forest is a rainforest that is on a mountainside. It is usually misty and cloudy.

CLIMAX VEGETATION

Climax vegetation is the final stage in the development of an area.

CLUB MOSSES

Club mosses (Lycopsids) are primitive, vascular plants (pteridophytes) that evolved over 375 million years ago (during the Devonian). Huge club mosses went extinct during the Permian mass extinction; smaller ones lived during the time of the dinosaurs. These plants live near moisture (in order for their spores to germinate). These fast-growing, resilient plants propagate with rhizomes (underground stems). Classification: Division Lycopodiophyta, Class Lycopodiopsida, Order Lycopodiales, Family Lycopodiaceae (Club-mosses).

COAL

Coal is a combustible mineral formed from organic matter (mostly plant material) that lived about 300 million years ago (during the Pennsylvanian Period). During the Pennsylvanian Period, the earth was covered with huge swampy forests of giant ferns, horsetails, and club mosses. As layer upon layer of these plants died, they were compressed and covered with soil, stopping the decomposition process, forming peat. Heat and pressure chemically forced out oxygen and hydrogen, leaving carbon-rich deposits, called coal. A 20-foot-thick layer of plant material produces a one-foot-thick layer (seam) of coal.

COLEOPTILE

A coleoptile is a protective sheath that surrounds the shoot tip and the embryonic leaves of the young shoot of grasses.

COMET

A comet is a celestial body that orbits around the sun. Its tail of gas and dust always points away from the sun.

COMMENSALISM

Commensalism is a situation in which two organisms are associated in a relationship in which one benefits from the relationship and the other is not affected much. The two animals are called commensals. An example of commensalism is bromeliads (plants living on trees in rainforests) and frogs; the frogs get shelter and water from the bromeliad but the bromeliad is unaffected. Commensalism is a type of symbiosis.

COMPANION CELL

A companion cell is a type of cell that pumps nutrients (sugars) into phloem cells.

COMPLETE FLOWER

A complete flower has a stamen, a pistil, petals, and sepals.

COMPOSITE FLOWER

A composite flower (like the sunflower) has a many individual flowers (called florets) on a wide, flat receptacle, that look like a single flower. The flowers in the central disk are called disk flowers; the flowers on the periphery are called ray flowers. This group is called Asteraceae (Compositae).

COMPOUND LEAF

A compound leaf is a leaf that is divided into many separate parts (leaflets) along a midrib (the rachis). All the leaflets of a compound leaf are oriented in the same plane. When a compound leaf falls from the tree, it falls as a unit. A double compound leaf is one in which each leaflet of a compound leaf is also made up of secondary leaflets.

CONE

A cone (strobilus) is the reproductive fruiting structure of many tracheophytes. It is a group of scales that are joined to a central stalk; the seeds are borne on the surface of the cone scales. A cone scale contains either ovules or spores (depending on whether it is female or male).

CONIFER

Most conifers are evergreen trees and shrubs that bear naked seeds in cones (a woody strobilus). Examples of modern-day conifers include pine, fir, larch, redwood, and spruce trees. Mesozoic era conifers included redwoods, yews, pines, the monkey puzzle tree (Araucaria), cypress, and Pseudofrenelopsis (a Cheirolepidiacean). Towards the end of the Mesozoic, flowering plants flourished and began to overtake conifers as the dominant flora.

CONSERVATION

Conservation is the wise use of natural resources (plants, animals, minerals, water, etc.) so that they are not damaged and will be in good condition in the future.

CONSUMER

A consumer is a living thing that eats other living things to survive. It cannot make its own food (unlike most plants, which are producers). Primary consumers eat producers, secondary consumers eat primary consumers, and so on. There are always many more primary consumers than secondary consumers, etc.

CONTINENTAL DRIFT

Continental drift is the movement of the earth's continents. The land masses are hunks of earth's crust that float on the molten core. The ideas of continental drift and the supercontinent of Pangaea were presented by A. Wegener in 1915.

CONTRACTILE ROOT

A contractile root is a root that contracts (gets smaller) and pulls down the crown of the plant below the surface of the soil.

CONVERGENT EVOLUTION

Convergent evolution (convergence) is when a trait develops independently in two or more groups of organisms. An example of convergence is the wings of Pterodactyls and bats.

COOKSONIA

Cooksonia is the oldest-known land plant. This primitive plant dates from Silurian period, about 428 million years ago Cooksonia was an erect plant with dichotomous branches and terminal sporangia (sacs that produce reproductive spores). Cooksonia fosils have been found in the USA, Canada, and Czechoslovakia.

COPPICE SHOOT

A coppice shoot (also called a epicormic shoot, sap shoot, water shoot, or water sprout) is a shoot (new growth) that arises from an adventitious or dormant bud on a branch or a stem of a plant (usually near the base of the plant). This fast-growing shoot often starts to grow when part of a forest canopy is removed or thinned (allowing light in).

COPPICE STAND

A coppice stand is an area of coppice shoots.

CORN

Corn is a cereal plant in the grass family. It an important agricultural plant native to Mexico or South America. It's scientific name is *Zea mays*. The edible part of corn in the kernels, rows of seeds that grow on an elongated ear covered by husks (specialized leaves).

CORPSE FLOWER

The "corpse flower" is the world's largest flower. This giant bloom is found in rainforests of Indonesia. It's scientific name is *Rafflesia arnoldi*. Rafflesia gives off a putrid smell that reminds people of rotting meat (this odor attracts its pollenators, beetles and flies), hence its nickname. Rafflesia's enormous flower is about 3 feet (1 m) across and weighs about 20 pounds (9 kilograms). The flower takes about a year to develop, then it blooms for about a week before dying. The flower has five wide orange petals (with pale dots) surrounding a spiked cup. Rafflesia has no stem, no roots, and no leaves. The flower is supported by fungus-like tissue that lives in another plant - the Tetrastigma vine.

COQUINA

Coquina is a type of limestone (a kind of sedimentary rock) that is mostly made of shells and shell fragments.

CORDATE LEAF

A cordate leaf has a heart shape, with the wide part towards the petiole.

CORK

Cork (also called periderm) is the soft, light-weight bark of the cork oak tree. This low-density material floats in water. Cork cells are made by cork cambium cells. Cork contains suberin, a waxy, water-proof material. Cork protects the tree from water loss and from insects and infections.

CORM

A corm is a fleshy underground stem of some plants. It looks like a bulb, but is solid (it is not formed in layers).

CORN

Corn (*Zea mays*), also called maize, is a type of cereal grass; it is an edible grain. This tall, annual plant has long, alternately-spaced blade-like leaves, and a strong, solid stem. A flowering plant, staminate (male) flowers grow on the tassels at the end of the main axis of the stem. The pistillate (female) inflorescence grows into the ear of corn, and is a spike having a thick axis paired spikelets in rows (each row of paired spikelets produces two rows of grain). The ear is covered by modified leaves, called husks or shucks. Corn evolved in the Americas, but has been brought all around the world by people; it is the second-largest food crop (behind wheat). Classification: Division Magnoliophyta (angioperms), Class Magnoliopsida (dicots), Class Liliopsida (monocots), Subclass Commelinidae (grasses, sedges and rushes), Order Cyperales, Family Poaceae (Gramineae) (grasses).

COROLLA

The corolla consists of the petals of a flower.

COTYLEDON

The cotyledon is the embryonic leaf within a seed. When a seed germinates, the cotyledon is the first leaf to grow. Monocots have one cotyledon; dicots have two cotyledons.

CRENATE

A crenate leaf has edges (margins) shaped like rounded teeth.

CRENOLATE

A crenolate leaf margin has edges that are shallow-toothed.

CRETACEOUS PERIOD

Dinosaurs were at their height during the Cretaceous period, 146-65 million years ago, and flowering plants spread and flourished. There was a mass extinction (the K-T mass extinction) at the end of the Cretaceous, marking the end of the dinosaurs and many other species of animals and plants.

CRISPED

Crisped leaves have a tighly curled margin. Parsley and kale leaves are crisped.

CRISTAE

(singular crista): The multiply-folded inner membrane of a cell's mitochondrion that are finger-like projections. The walls of the cristae are the site of the cell's energy production (it is where ATP is generated).

CROSS-POLLINATION

Cross-pollination is the transfer of pollen from the anther to the stigma of a flower on a different plant.

CROWN

The crown of a plant is the area from which new shoots arise or the point at which the roots meet the stem. Also, the upper area of the tree that has a lot of branching and leaves.

CROZIER

The crozier is the spirally coiled "fiddlehead" of a young fern leaf.

CRYPTOGAM

Cryptogams are plants and plant-like organisms that do not reproduce with seeds and do not produce flowers. Many cryptogams reproduce using spores. Ferns, mosses, fungi, and algae are cryptogams.

CRYSTALS

Crystals are solids whose atoms form a very regular pattern.

CULM

A culm is the elongated straw or hollow stem of grasses. The culm usually supportes the inflorescence.

CULTIVAR

A cultivar is a plant that is a cultivated (bred) variety.

CUNEATE

Cuneate means wedge-shaped.

CUTICLE

The cuticle is the fatty or waxy outer layer of epidermal cells that are above ground.

CYANOBACTERIA

Cyanobacteria Blue-green algae (also called blue-green algae) are simple, (usually) one-celled photosynthetic organisms that lack a membrane-bound nucleus (they are prokaryotic). They belong to the kingdom Monera.

CYCAD

Cycads (Cycadophyta) are primitive seed plants that dominated the Jurassic period (cycads comprised 20% of the world flora). Cycads are palm-like trees that live in warm climates. Separate male and female plants exist (they are dioecious). These gymnosperms have long, divided leaves and produce large cones. Cycads evolved during the Pennsylvanian, had their heyday during the Mesozoic, and only about 185 species (in 11 genera) still exist today. Leptocycas (shown above) and Ptilophyllum were Mesozoic Era cycads. Later cycads had a more rounded, barrel-like base. Classifcation: Division Pinophyta (Gymnosperms), Subdivision Cycadicae, Class Cycadopsida, Order Cycadales, Family Cycadaceae (Cycads)

CYCADEOID

Cycadeoids (Bennettitales) were plants with woody stems (some erect, some spherical) and very tough leaves. Cycadeoids do not always have separate male and female plants. Cycadeoids are now extinct. Some Mesozoic Cycadeoids included: Cycadeoidea, Vardekloeftia, Williamsonia (shown above), Williamsoniella, Westersheimia, and Leguminanthus.

CYCADOPHYTES

Cycadophytes included the Cycads and Cycadeoids (Bennettitales), plants with woody stems (some erect, some spherical) and very tough leaves. These two groups differ mainly in the way they reproduce: Cycads have separate male and female plants; Cycadeoids do not always. Cycadeoids are now extinct but there are still a few cycads. Some Mesozoic Era Cycads included: Leptocycas, Cycas, Zamia, Dioon, Bowenia, Stangeria, and Microcyas. Some Mesozoic Cycadeoids included: Cycadeoidea, Vardekloeftia, Williamsonia, Williamsoniella, Westersheimia, and Leguminanthus.

CYME

A cyme is an inflorescence where the central flower opens first.

CYTOPLASM

Cytoplasm is the jelly-like material outside the cell nucleus in which the organelles are located (the entire contents of the cell located inside the plasma membrane, but excluding the nucleus).

CYTOSKELETON

The cytoskeleton is a network of protein filaments and microtubules that are located in the cytoplasm of eukaryotic cell, just under the cell membrane. The cytoskeleton acts as a support for the cell, as a spatial organizer, and as a channel for some chemical transport.

CYTOSOL

Cytoplasm is the jelly-like material in cells, excluding the cell nucleus and all organelles (the entire contents of the cell located inside the plasma membrane, but excluding the nucleus and other organelles).

D

DATING FOSSILS

Dating a fossil is determining when that organism was alive. Paleontologists use many ways of dating individual fossils in geologic time, including stratigraphy, observations of the fluctuations of the earth's magnetic field, radioisotope-dating, and looking at nearby index fossils.

DECIDUOUS

Deciduous plants lose their leaves seasonally, usually for the dry season. Some deciduous plants include ash, beech, hickory, maple, and oak.

DECOMPOSER

Decomposers are organisms like fungi and some bacteria that break down and digest the remains of organisms.

DECOMPOSITION

Decomposition is the decay or breakdown of things into more basic elements. For example, after a plant dies, it decomposes into organic nutrients.

DEFORESTATION

Deforestation is the loss of forest. Deforestation has many causes, including man's cutting down trees, forest fires, severe drought, changes in sea level, disease, etc.

DEHISCENT

A dehiscent is a structure on some plants that opens to release seeds or pollen grains.

DEHISCENT FRUIT

A dehiscent fruit splits open when it is maturite, causing the dispersal of its seeds. Some dehiscent fruits include cotton, poppy, peanuts, milkweed, magnolia, and all beans.

DEHYDRATE

To dehydrate is to lose a lot of water. Plants can become dehydrated in dry, hot weather.

DENDROCHRONOLOGY

Dendrochronology is the science in which tree rings are studied to determine conditions in the past.

DENDROCLIMATOLOGY

Dendroclimatology is the science in which tree rings are studied to determine climate changes in the past.

DESERT

A desert is a very dry area that receives less than 10 inches (25 cm) of rainfall each year. Desert organisms have adapted to life with little water.

DETRIVORE

A detrivore (or detritus feeder) is an organism that eats the dead remains of other organisms (detritus). Examples of detrivores include some bacteria and fungi.

DIASPORE

A diaspore (also called a disseminule) is a part of a plant that is separated from the plant and dispersed (sent or taken away from the plant) for reproduction. Diaspora include seeds, fruits, and spores.

DICHOTOMOUS KEY

A dichotomous key is a method for determining the identity of sometihing (like a butterfly, a plant, or a rock) by going through a series of choices that lead the user to the correct name of the item. At each step of the process, the user is given two choices; each alternative leads to another questions until the identification is completed. For example, a question in a dichotomous key for trees might be something like, "Does it have flat or needle-like leaves?" Dichotomous means "divided in two parts".

DICHOTOMOUS VENATION

Dichotomous venation is a pattern of leaf veins in which the veins branch in two over and over again. Ferns are dichotomousy veined. A few angiosperms and gymnosperms (like gingkos) have dichotomous venation.

DICOT

A dicot (Class Magnoliopsida) is a type of flowering plant (an angiosperm) whose seed has two embryonic leaves (cotyledons). The leaf veins are usually net-like (and not parallel). Taproots are often present. Beans and peas are examples of dicots.

DICTYOSTELE

A dictyostele is a siphonostele (a cylinder of vascular tissue) that has two or more overlapping leaf gaps (as in ferns). It is a divided stele located in the outer cortex (instead of in the center of the stem). Dictyosteles are composed of individual vascular bundles.

DIMORPHISM

Dimorphism means having two forms. It usually means that an organism has two different types, for example, males and females of some species look different, and are said to be sexually dimorphic.

DIOECIOUS

A dioecious plant has the male and female flowers on different plants. For example, date trees are dioecious.

DIPLOID

A diploid cell has the same number of chromosomes that most other cells of that organism have (except the gametes, like the sperm and the egg, which are haploid).

DIRT

Dirt is another name for soil. Soil is a natural, constantly-changing substance that is made up of minerals, organic materials, and living organisms. Plants grow in soil.

DISPERSAL

Dispersal is the process in which an organism spreads out geographically. Seeds are dispersed by the winds and by animals.

DISPERSERS

Dispersers are animals that spread plant seeds. Some dispersers include birds, insects, bats, and furry animals like monkeys.

DISSEMINULE

A disseminule (also called a diaspore) is a part of a plant that is separated from the plant and dispersed (sent or taken away from the plant) for reproduction. Dissemules include seeds, fruits, and spores.

DNA

DNA (short for deoxyribonucleic acid) is a complex organic molecule that carries the genetic information of an organism. DNA is the primary constituent of chromosomes. DNA is made up of two strands of amino acid bases (adenosine, cytosine, guanine, and thymine) arranged in a double helix. DNA's chemical instructions are carried to throughout the cell by another nucleotide, RNA.

DOGGER EPOCH

The Dogger epoch was the middle part of the Jurassic period, about 180 to 159 million years ago.

DOMINANT

The dominant plant is the most adundant species in an area, for example, pine trees are dominant in a pine forest.

DORMANCY

Dormancy is a period in which a plant has no active growth in response to harsh environmental conditions (like droughts or cold seasons).

DOUBLE COMPOUND LEAF

A double compound leaf is a leaf in which each leaflet of a compound leaf is made up of secondary leaflets.

DRIP TIP

The drip tip is the long, sharply-pointed tip on some rainforest plant leaves that allows water to flow quickly off the leaf surface. In the rainforest, many leaves have a drip tip. Without it, water would build up on the leaf.

E

EARTH

The earth is the third planet from the sun.

ECOSYSTEM

An ecosystem is the interrelationships between all of the living things in an area.

EDICARA FAUNA

Ediacara fauna is the animal life that lived during the Vendian or Ediacaran period (roughly 650 to 544 million years ago). The Vendian is when the earliest-known animals evolved. Vendian biota (Ediacara fauna), included soft-bodied multi-cellular animals, like sponges, cnidarians, worms, and soft-bodied relatives of the arthropods. The Ediacara was named for the Ediacara Hills in Australia, north of Adelaide, where these early animal fossils were first found (in 1946, by the Australian mining geologist Reginald C. Sprigg). Other Vendian Period fossils have been found in Mistaken Point, Newfoundland and the White Sea off the northern coast of Russia.

EMBRYO

An embryo is a developing plant still inside the seed. The embryo has cotyledons (embryonic leaves), a root cap, a food source and a plumule (shoot), all located inside the protective seed coat.

EMERGENTS

Emergents are giant trees in a rainforest that are much higher (up to 270 feet or 81 m) than the average canopy height. The emergents house many birds and insects in a very dry environment.

ENDANGERED SPECIES

An endangered species is a group of organisms that is dwindling in numbers and may go extinct soon. Many species of plants are endangered.

ENDEMIC

Endemic plants are native to an area and are only found in that area.

ENDOPLASMIC RETICULUM

The endoplasmic reticulum (ER) is a network of membranes in plant cells (and all eukaryotic cells) that control protein synthesis and cellular organization.

ENTIRE

An entire leaf has smooth edges (margins) with neither teeth nor lobes.

EON

Two or more geological eras form an Eon, which is the largest division of geological time, lasting hundreds of millions of years.

Eon	**Time**
Phanerozoic Eon	540 million years ago through today
Proterozoic Eon	2.5 billion years ago to 540 million years ago
Archaeozoic Eon	3.9 to 2.5 billion years ago
Hadean Eon	4.6 to 3.9 billion years ago

EPHEMERALS

Ephemerals are plants that have an accelerated life cycle. These hardy plants grow and reproduce quickly - they are often dormant during extreme weather (droughts, heat spells, cold spells, etc.). Their seeds are drought resistant. These plants often live in areas with harsh climates, like deserts and very cold areas. Some ephemerals include: Desert Paintbrush, Desert Sand Verbena, Dutchman's Breeches, Mojave Aster, and Yellow Trout Lily.

EPICORMIC SHOOT

An epicormic shoot (also called a coppice shoot, sap shoot, water shoot, or water sprout) is a shoot (new growth) that arises from an adventitious or dormant bud on a branch or a stem of a plant (usually near the base of the plant). This fast-growing shoot often starts to grow when part of a forest canopy is removed or thinned (allowing light in).

EPICOTYL

The epicotyl is the part of the stem that is above the first leaves.

EPIDERMIS

The epidermis is the outer protective layer of a plant. This tissue helps prevent injury and minimizes water loss by evaporation.

EPIGYNOUS OVARY

An epigynous ovary (also called an inferior ovary) is an ovary located below the flower parts (the calyx, corolla, and androecium). The flower parts are attached to the top of the ovary.

EPIPHYTE

Epiphytes are plants that live attached to a plant (or other structure like a rock, telephone pole or a building) and not in the ground). Epiphytes include many orchids and bromeliads. Epiphytes are not parasites; they get water and nutrients from the air (and not their host).

EPOCH

An epoch is a division of a geologic period; it is the smallest division of geologic time, lasting several million years.

EQUATORIAL RAINFOREST

Tropical rainforests are warm, very wet forests that do not freeze (the temperature remains over 75°F=24°C) and do not get extremely hot. Tropical rainforests cover about 7% of the earth's surface, in a band around the equator. They are also called tropical rainforests.

EQUISETUM

Equisetum, a modern genus of horsetail is a primitive, spore-bearing plant (a sphenopsid) with rhizomes. Its side branches are arranged in rings along the hollow stem. Other genera of horsetail were common during the Mesozoic Era, like Neocalamites, Calamites etc. Horsetails date from the Devonian period 408-360 million years ago, but are still around today and are invasive weeds.

ERA

Two or more geological periods comprise an era, which is hundreds of millions of years in duration.

ETHNOBOTANY

Ethnobotany is the science which studies how plants are used in various cultures.

EUKARYOTE

A eukaryote (which means "true nucleus") is an organism whose cells have internal membranes (which divide the cell into regions that have different functions) and a structurally-discrete nucleus. They also have a cytoskeleton which controls their shape. Eukaryotes include plants, animals, fungi, and protists (they do not include blue-green algae, bacteria, viruses, and other primitive microorganisms).

EURASIA

Eurasia is the combined, joined land masses of Europe and Asia.

EUTROPHICATION

Eutrophication is when the concentration of nutrients in a waterway increases; this occurs when sewage, fertilizers, or sediments enter the water. This increase in the concentration of nitrogen and/or phosphorous may result in an algal bloom (an overabundance of blue-green algae that depletes the water of oxygen, killing other organisms).

EVAPORATION

Evaporation is the process in which a liquid is transferred into gaseous form.

EVAPOTRANSPIRATION

Evapotranspiration is the process in which rain water evaporates from trees and returns to the atmosphere.

EVERGLADES

The Everglades is a swamp located in southwestern Florida. It contains over 2,000 different types of plants, including saw grass (Cladium jamaicense), mangroves (including the red, black and white mangroves), alligator flag (Thalia geniculata), strangler fig (Ficus aurea), gumbo-limbo (Bursera simaruba), mahogany (Swietenia mahagoni), saw palmetto, pond cypress (Taxodium ascendens), bald cypress (Taxodium distichum), moonvine (a morning glory), coontie, and various willows, slash pine (Pinus elliottii densa) and other pines, and oaks with Spanish moss hanging form the limbs. Many epiphytes (air plants) like the night-blooming epidendrum (Epidendrum nocturnum) also live in trees.

EVERGREEN

Evergreen plants do not lose their leaves seasonally. Pines and firs are examples of evergreens.

EVOLUTION

Evolution is a process in which the gene pool of a population gradually (over millions of years) changes in response to environmental pressures, natural selection, and genetic mutations. All forms of life came into being by this process.

EVOLVE

To evolve is to develop by the process of evolution, changing in some way as an adaptation to the environment.

EXTINCT

An animal species that is extinct has died out. Most animal species that ever existed have gone extinct, including all the dinosaurs.

EXTINCTION

Extinction is the process in which groups of organisms (species) die out.

EXTINCTION-LEVEL EVENT

An Extinction-Level Event is a catastrophic event (such as a large asteroid or comet hitting the earth, a large change in the earth's temperature/sea level, tremendously increased volcanism, etc.) that is capable of causing a mass extinction. This event would greatly damage the ecosphere of earth, causing many groups of organisms to die.

EXTRACTIVE RESERVE

An extractive reserve is an area in a rain forest in which people are allowed to harvest crops, such as rubber or Brazil nuts.

EYE

An eye is an axillary bud on an underground plant part such as a tuber (e.g., potato) or in the area where the stem joins the tuberous root (e.g., dahlia).

F

FAMILY

In classification, a family is a group of related or similar organisms. A family contains one or more genera (plural of genus). A group of similar families forms an order.

FAST PLANTS

Fast Plants are fast-growing plant varieties that were developed at the University of Wisconsin, Madison, Wisconsin, USA. Fast Plants complete their life cycles about 45 days after planting. Fast plants are used in classrooms and laboratories around the world for teaching and research. The first plants in space were Fast Plants.

FEN

A fen is a wet area rich in peat and other organic matter.

FERN

Ferns are non-flowering vascular plants with rhizomes that were plentiful during the Mesozoic Era and usually live in warm, moist areas. Ferns have fronds divided into leaflets. Classification: Plyla: Lycophyta (lower ferns like clubmosses), Pterophyta (ferns), Psilophyta (whisk ferns) (true ferns belong to the Class Filices).

FERTILIZER

Fertilizer is material that is added to soil to increase is fertility and output. Fertilizers include manure, compost, and chemical mixtures.

FIBROUS ROOT

A fibrous root is a type of primary root of a plant that has a lot of side branching. Fibrous root are the most common type of roots.

FILAMENT

The filament is the part of the flower that holds the anther.

FLAGELLUM

A flagellum is a long, thin, whip-like structure that is found on some organisms, including some unicellular algae. Flagella help propel the organism through water.

FLAX

Flax (family Linaceae, genus Linum) is a flowering plant from cool, temperate areas. It has narrow, lance-shaped leaves and blue flowers - the plant grow to be up to about 1.5 to 2 feet tall. Flax is grown for its seeds (which yield oil) and linen fiber (a strong vegetable fiber that is made from the woody stalk of the flax plant).

FLORA

The flora is all the plants that live in an area.

FLOWER

The flower is the reproductive unit of angiosperms. Flowers usually have carpels, petals, sepals, and stamens. Some flowers (called perfect flowers) have both male and female reproductive organs; some flowers (called imperfect flowers) have only male reproductive organs (stamens) or only female reproductive organs (ovary, style, and stigma). Some plants have both male and female flowers, while other have males on one plant and females on another. Complete flowers have a stamen, a pistil, petals, and sepals. Incomplete flowers lack one of these parts.

FLOWERING PLANTS

Flowering plants are angiosperms (meaning "covered seed"). They produce seeds enclosed in fruit (an ovary). They are the dominant type of plant today; there are over

250,000 species, including grasses, peas, etc. Their flowers are used in reproduction. Angiosperms evolved about 140 million years ago, during the late Jurassic period, and were eaten by dinosaurs. They became the dominant land plants about 100 million years ago (edging out conifers, a type of gymnosperm). Angiosperms are divided into the monocots (like corn) and dicots (like beans).

FOLIAGE

Foliage is the leaves of plants.

FOLIVORE

A folivore is animal that eats foliage (leaves). For example, the green iguana is a folivore.

FOOD WEB

A food chain is the sequence of who eats whom in a biological community (an ecosystem) to obtain nutrition. A food web is all of the interactions between predators and prey in which plants and animals obtain food in an ecoystem. The web starts with plants or other autotrophs (organisms that make their own food from light and/or chemical energy) that are eaten by herbivores (plant-eaters). The herbivores are eaten by carnivores (meat-eaters). These are eaten by other carnivores. When any organism dies, it is eaten by tiny microbes (detrivores) and the exchange of energy continues.

FORB

A forb is a small, herbaceous (non-woody), broad-leaved vascular plant (excluding grasses, rushes, sedges, etc.). For example, wild flowers are a type of forb.

FOREST

A forest is an area in which trees are the dominant plant.

FOREST FLOOR

The forest floor is the lowest layer of a rainforest, extending from the ground to about 3 feet (1 m) high. This layer is teeming with animal life, especially insects. The largest animals in the rainforest generally live here.

FOREST SUCCESSION

Forest or plant succession is the natural pattern of ecosystem growth and change over time for a particular environment. Plant life follows established patterns of growth and change after major distruptions, like fires, floods, agricultural damage, logging, etc. Generally, smaller, fast-growing herbaceous species and grasses grow first in an open field, followed in a few years by softwood tree seedlings and larger herbaceous species. As a young forest develops into a mature forest (30 to 70 years), an understory of smaller hardwood trees develops. The final stage is a climax hardwood forest (100 plus years).

FOSSIL

Fossils are mineralized impressions or casts of ancient animals and plants. Fossils have been found on every continent on the earth.

FOSSIL FUEL

A fossil fuel is a naturally-ocurring, energy-rich organic (carbon-based) substance (like shale, petroleum (oil), coal, or natural gas) in the earth's crust that was formed from ancient organic material (mostly plants).

FROND

A frond is the fern-like (or feathery) foliage of a plant that has many divisions. Ferns and palms have fronds. Frond is also used to refer to the main part of a kelp plant (excluding the holdfast).

FRUIT

A fruit is the part of a flowering plant that contains the seeds. Some fruits include apples, oranges, berries, maple pods, and acorns. Some fruit are fleshy and some are dry, like cotton (a dehiscent fruit) and sunflower (an indehiscent fruit). Not all fruit are edible. True (simple) fruits (like the tomato, coconut, watermelon, olive, lemon, and banana) develop from the wall of a single ovary. False (compound) fruits (like the strawberry, rosehip, and pineapple) develop from more than one pistil.

FUNGUS

Fungus (plural fungi) are organisms that obtain energy by breaking down dead organic material and that produce spores. Some fungi include mushrooms, toadstools, slime molds, yeast, penicillin, mold, and mildew. Classification: kingdom Fungus.

G

GALLIC EPOCH

The Gallic epoch was the middle part of the Cretaceous period, about 127 million to 89 million years ago.

GAMETANGIUM

A gametangium is a reproductive organ that is in some plants (especially algae, fungi, mosses, and ferns). The gametangium produces gametes (reproductive cells).

GAMETE

A gamete is the male or female reproductive cell of an organism (the sperm or the egg). Each gamete has only half the number of chromosomes that the other cells of that organism have. It is haploid.

GASTROLITHS

Gastroliths are stones that some animals swallow and use to help grind up tough plant matter in their digestive system. They're also called gizzard rocks.

GENOME

The genome of an organism is made up of the set of chromosomes that contain all of its genes.

GENUS

In classification, a genus is a group of related or similar organisms. A genus contains one or more species. A group of similar genera (the plural of genus) forms a family. In the scientific name of an organism, the first name is its genus (for example, people are *Homo sapiens* - our genus is *Homo* and our species is *H. Sapiens*).

GEOLOGICAL TIME

The history of the earth is described in geological time, which is measured in millions of years and billions of years. The divisions used are: eon, era, period, and epoch.

GEOLOGICAL TIME PERIODS

Geologic time is divided into divisions based on some distinguishing feature of that time (like an Ice Age). The divisions used are: eon, era, period, epoch, and age.

GEOLOGY

Geology is the study of the earth's structure, including rocks.

GEOTROPISM

Geotropism is a plant's reaction to gravity in which the roots go towards the pull of gravity, and the shoots go in the opposite direction.

GERMINATION

Germination is the beginning of growth of a plant from its seed.

GIGANTOPTERID

Gigantopterids were ancient seed plants that lived during the Permian period, over 250 million years ago. It is thought that the gigantopterids evolved into the flowering plants. One species of gigantopterid is the broad-leafed climbing plant *Vasovinea tianiia*; it was found in 1993 in China.

GINKGO or GINGKO

Ginkgo or Gingko also called the maidenhair tree is a primitive seed-bearing tree (a gymnosperm) that was common during the Mesozoic Era, but has only one existing species now. Ginkgos peaked during the Jurassic and Cretaceous periods. This deciduous (losing its leaves in cold weather) tree has fan-shaped leaves divided into two lobes. Classification: Division Pinophyta (Gymnosperms),

Subdivision Pinicae, Class Pinopsida, Order Ginkgoales, Family Ginkgoaceae (ginkgos).

GIZZARD ROCKS

Gizzard rocks are stones that some animals swallow and use to help grind up tough plant matter in their digestive system. They're also called gastroliths.

GLABROUS

A glabrous surface lacks hairs (and has a smooth surface).

GLOCHID

Glochids are tufts of short, barbed spines that are found at the areoles of opuntia cacti.

GLOSSOPTERIS

Glossopteris (from the Greek glossa, meaning tongue, because the leaves were tongue shaped) is a genus of extinct seed fern (a Pteriosperm) whose fossils are found throughout India, South America, southern Africa, Australia, and Antarctica. Glossopteris was about 12 ft (3.6 m) tall. The distribution of this fossil plant throughout the southern hemisphere led the Austrian geologist Eduard Suess to deduce that there had once been a land bridge between these areas. He named this large land mass Gondwanaland (named after a district in India where the plant Glossopteris was found). This was the southern supercontinent formed after Pangaea broke up during the Jurassic period. It included what are now the continents South America, Africa, India, Australia, and Antarctica. These deciduous (losing their leaves in the cool season) gymnosperms arose during the late Permian and became dominant, but went extinct by the end of the Triassic period.

GOLGI BODY

Also called the Golgi apparatus or Golgi complex, a flattened, layered, sac-like organelle that looks like a stack of pancakes and is located near the nucleus. It produces the membranes that surround the lysosomes. The Golgi body packages proteins and carbohydrates into membrane-bound vesicles for "export" from the cell.

GONDWANALAND

Gondwanaland, also known as Gondwana, was the southern supercontinent formed after Pangaea broke up during the Jurassic period. It included what are now the continents South America, Africa, India, Australia, and Antarctica. Gondwanaland was named for a district in India where the fossil plant Glossopteris was found; this plant led E. Suess to deduce that the southern continents were once joined, supporting Wegener's continental drift theory.

GRAFT

A graft is a shoot or bud that has been joined to another plant.

GRAIN

A grain is a single particle of pollen.

GRANUM

(plural grana) A stack of thylakoid disks within the chloroplast is called a granum.

GRASS

Grasses are a group of flowering plants (angiosperms) that belong to the family Graminae. Classification: Division Magnoliophyta (angioperms), Class Magnoliopsida (dicots), Class Liliopsida (monocots), Subclass Commelinidae (grasses, sedges and rushes, Order Cyperales, Family Poaceae (Gramineae) (grasses).

GRAZER

A grazer is an animal that eats low-lying vegetation, such as grasses and other low plants.

GRAZING FOOD CHAIN

The grazing food chain is a model that describes the flow of organic energy through organisms in an ecosystem. A trophic level is a level of this grazing food chain. Plants (called primary producers) occupy the first trophic level. Plant-eaters (also called primary consumers) occupy the second trophic level in the grazing food chain. The third level contains animals that eat primary consumers (first-level carnivores = secondary consumers). The fourth trophic level contains tertiary consumers, generally larger animals (like eagles) that eat primary consumers.

GREENHOUSE EFFECT

The greenhouse effect is an increase in the temperature of a planet as heat energy from sunlight is trapped in the atmosphere. Excess carbon dioxide and water vapor increase this effect. The greenhouse effect is strong on the earth, maintaining and possible exacerbating warm temperatures.

GREEN REVOLUTION

The green revolution was a dramatic increase in agricultural yields that occurred in the 1950s through 1960s. The green revolution was based upon many improvements in plant science, including the genetic improvement of many plants (including new, high-yield hybrid varieties), improved irrigation, more efficient machinery, new fertilizers, and pest controls that increased plants' disease-resistance, improved their hardiness, and increased their productivity (especially rice, wheat, and corn).

GUARD CELL

Each stoma has two crescent-shaped guard cells that control the size of the opening of the stoma using turgor pressure. This changes the amount of water vapor and other gases that can enter and leave the plant.

GUM

Gum is a sticky substance that is secreted by some plants. Gum hardens when it dries.

GYMNOSPERM

Gymnosperms (meaning "naked seeds") are seed-bearing plants that don't produce flowers. These plants release pollen into the air to the female ovule, causing fertilization. Their seeds develop without a protective covering. The earliest gymnosperms were seed ferns from the Devonian period (408-360 million years ago). Some examples of gymnosperms are conifers (like pines, redwoods, and fir), gingkos, seed ferns, cycadeoids, and cycads. These plants were very important to plant-eating dinosaurs.

H

HABITAT

A habitat is a space (which includes food, water and shelter) suitable for the survival and reproduction of an organism.

HALF-LIFE

The half-life of a radioisotope is the amount of time it takes for half of the radioisotope to decay.

HALOMORPHIC

Halomorphic characteristics are adaptations to a saline (salt water) environments.

HALOPHTYE

A halophyte is a plant that has adapted to salty soils.

HAPLOID

A haploid cell has only half the number of chromosomes that the other cells of that organism have (most are diploid). Gametes (like the sperm and the egg) are haploid.

HARDWOOD

Hardwood trees are trees whose wood is dense, strong, and relativel non-absorbent of water. These slow-growing trees include oak and maple. Hardwood trees have broad leaves and not needles.

HARDY

A hardy plant is one that can withstand the extremes of climate, like frost.

HAUSTORIAL ROOT

An haustorial root is one that absorbs water and nutrients from another plant (and not the soil).

HEATH

A heath is an area of open land that is covered with low-growing shrubs like heather.

HECTARE

A hectare is metric unit of area. A hectare is equal to 10,000 square meters.

HERB

An herb is a seed plant that does not have a woody stem. Every year, herbaceous plants produce a completely new stem. Herbaceous plants are generally short lived and relatively short (compared to woody plants). Some herbaceous plants include the banana, grasses, and forbs.

HERBICIDE

An herbicide is a chemical that kills certain plants. Herbicides are usually intended to kill weeds.

HERB LAYER

The herb layer is another name for the floor of a rainforest.

HERBIVORE

Herbivores (also called primary consumers) are animals that eat plants.

HERMAPHRODITE

A hermaphrodite is a plant that has both female and male reproductive organs.

HETEROTROPH

A heterotroph (also called a consumer) is a living thing that eats other living things to survive. It cannot make its own food (unlike plants, which are autotrophs, making their own food). Animals are heterotrophs.

HETEROPHYLLOUS

A heterophyllous (meaning "other leaf") plant or branch has two or more different leaf shapes on it. Although these leaves have different shapes, they have similar internal anatomical organizations.

HILUM

The hilum is the scar on a seed coat at the location where it was attached to the plant's stalk during development.

HOLDFAST

A holdfast is the root-like structure of kelp that holds the base of the plant in place on the sea floor. Unlike real roots, however, the holdfast does not obtain and supply nutrients to the rest of the plant.

HOMOLOGY

Homology is the similarity of characters found in different species that are due to common descent. Examples include the flippers of whales and our arms.

HOMOPLASY

Homoplasy is the similarity of characters found in different species that are not from common descent. Examples include the wings of insects and the wings of pterosaurs. These characters derive from convergent evolution, parallel evolution, or character reversal.

HORMONE

A hormone is a chemical in plants (and other organisms) that regulates the plant's growth, reproduction, and other functions.

HORSETAIL

Horsetail is a primitive, spore-bearing plant (a sphenopsid and a pteridophyte) with rhizomes that was common during the Mesozoic Era. Its side branches are arranges in rings along the hollow stem. Horsetails date from the Devonian period 408-360 million years ago, but are still around today and are invasive weeds. Classification: Division Equisetophyta, Class Equisetopsida, Order Equisetales, Family Equisetaceae (Horsetails).

HORTICULTURE

Horticulture is the science of growing fruits, vegetables, flowers, and ornamental plants.

HOST

A host is an organism which a parasite uses for food and/ or shelter.

HUMUS

Humus is the rich, organic portion of the soil. It is composed of decayed plant and animal materials.

HUXLEY, THOMAS H.

Thomas H. Huxley (1825-1895) was a British scientist and friend of Charles Darwin. He was the first scientist to notice the similarity between birds and dinosaurs. He named: Acanthopholis (1865), the family Archaeopteryglidae (1871), Euskelosaurus (1866), Hypsilophodon (1869), and the family Megalosauridae (1869).

HYBRID

A hybrid is the offspring of two organisms that belong to different breeds, varieties, species or genera.

HYDRIC

Hydric environmental conditions are ones that are very wet.

HYDROLOGIC CYCLE

The Hydrologic Cycle (also known as the water cycle) is the journey water takes as it circulates from the earth to the sky and back again.

HYDROPHYTE

A hydrophyte is a plant that grows in water or in water-logged soil. Hydrophytes have a reduced root system, reduced support and vascular systems, and specialized leaves. Some hydrophytic plants include waterliles and Wolffia (which is the smallest flowering plant). Anchored hydrophytes have a rooting system that is embedded in the soil and they often have floating leaves.

HYDROPONICS

Hydroponics is a method of growing plants in water that contains dissolved nutrients.

HYOPOCOTYL

The hypocotyl is the part of the stem of a sprouting plant that is above the root and below the stalk of the cotyledons (seed leaves).

I

ICE AGE

An ice age is a time lasting thousands of years during which the earth is very cold and largely covered by ice and glaciers.

ICHNITES

Also known as trace fossils or ichnofossils, these are fossilized footprints, nests, dung, gastroliths, burrows, stomach contents, etc., but not actual body parts. Ichnofossils record the movement and behavior of animals. Ichnology is the study of ichnites.

ICHNOFOSSILS

Also known as trace fossils or ichnites, these are fossilized footprints, nests, dung, gastroliths, burrows, stomach contents, etc., but not actual body parts. Ichnofossils record the movement and behavior of animals. Ichnology is the study of ichnofossils.

IGNEOUS ROCK

When molten rock cools, igneous rock is formed.

IMBIBITION

Imbibition is the process in which a seed takes up water from its surrounding and swells. This powerful process precedes germination and can spit the seed coat.

IMPACT CRATER

Impact craters are the remains of collisions between an asteroid, comet, or meteorite and the earth.

IMPERFECT FLOWER

An imperfect flower has either male (stamen) and female (ovary) reproductive organs on the same flower, but not both.

INCOMPLETE FLOWER

An incomplete flower is missing one of the four major parts of the flower, the stamen, pistil, petals, or sepals.

INDEHISCENT

A fruit that remains closed at maturity is indehiscent. Nuts, acorns, sunflowers, grains, and maple pods are examples of indehiscent fruits.

INDEX FOSSILS

Index fossils are commonly found fossils that are limited in time span. They help in dating other fossils. For example: trilobites were common during the Paleozoic, but not found before the Permian period, and ammonites were common during the Mesozoic Era, but not found after the Cretaceous period. Another example: the oldest-known ostracods are from the Cambrian period; they became widespread during the Ordovician and remain so.

INDIGENOUS

An indigenous organism is one that lives naturally in a particular region and were not introduced there by man.

INFERIOR OVARY

An inferior ovary (also called an epigynous ovary) is an ovary located below the flower parts (the calyx, corolla, and androecium). The flower parts are attached to the top of the ovary.

INFLORESCENCE

Inflorescence is the a type of flower in which there is more that one flower in a single structure.

INSECTIVOROUS

Insectivorous organisms eat insects. Insectivorous plants trap and digest insects for nourishment.

INSECTS

Insects have exoskeletons and six legs. They evolved during the Silurian Period, 438 to 408 million years ago, long before dinosaurs existed.

INTERNODE

The part of a plant's stem between two nodes is the internode—the distance along the stem between the leaves.

INTERSPECIFIC COMPETITION

Interspecific competition is competition between two different species of organisms (competing for food, water, territory, etc.).

INTRASPECIFIC COMPETITION

Intraspecific competition is competition among members of a species (competing for food, water, territory, etc.).

IRIDIUM

Iridium is a heavy metal element that is rare on the earth's surface, but abundant on chondritic meteors and in the earth's core.

IRIDIUM ANOMALY

The iridium anomaly is a layer of earth's crust (the K-T layer, which is about 65 million years old) in which there is excess of iridium (a relatively rare element). The presence of this extra Iridium supports the Alvarez asteroid theory, since this iridium may have come from an asteroid.

IRRADIANCE

Irradiance is the amout of light energy from the Sun that hits the earth in an area.

ISOTOPE

An isotope of an element is another form of the same element that has a different number of neutrons in the nucleus (giving it a different atomic weight).

J

JUNGLE

A jungle is a rainforest or a forest whose canopy trees have been logged (cut), causing lush growth on the forest floor (also known as a secondary forest).

JUNIPER

Junier is a conifer and a gymnosperm with blue, woody fruits and overlapping, scale-like leaves. Classification: division Coniferophyta, family Cupressaceae.

JURASSIC PERIOD

Birds evolved and many dinosaurs flourished during the Jurassic period, 208-146 million years ago. Flowering plants appeared about 140 million years ago, during the late Jurassic period.

JUVENILE

A juvenile plant is in an early phase of plant growth in which it increases in size but has not yet flowered.

K

KAPOK TREE

The kapok tree, *Ceiba pentandra* or *Eriodendron anfractuosum*, is a large, deciduous, tropical tree that is native to tropical America, Africa, and the East Indies. This fast-growing tree is generally from 45 to over 100 feet (14-30 m) tall; the kapok is the tallest tree in Africa. It has pink, white, or yellow flowers in clusters. The light-weight silky down from the seed pods (sometimes called Java cotton) is used as pillow stuffing, sleeping bag stuffing, life jacket stuffing, furniture upholstery, insulation, and for other uses. The green leaves are lanceolate (lance shaped) and palmately compound (with 5 to 9 leaflets). The yellow-green oil from the seeds is used in foods and to manufacture soap. Young leaves are also cooked and eaten; the wood is also used. The night-blooming flowers are pollinated and the seeds are spread by fruit bats.

KELP

Kelp is a cold-water seaweed that belongs to the family Laminariaceae. It is a large, floating plant that grows in large masses (called kelp forests) and is held to the sea floor by a holdfast. Kelp is usually brown. This seaweed is used by people as food, a food additive, fertilizer (when reduced to ash), and as an ingredient in many other products. Kelp evolved during in the Miocene epoch. Kelp is included in either kingdom Protista or Chromista.

KELP FOREST

A kelp forest is a marine ecosystem (a biome) that is dominated by large kelp plants. These oceanic forests grow in cold and temperate waters, especially along the western coasts of the continents.

KINGDOM

In classification, a kingdom is the highest grouping of similar organisms. A kingdom contains one or more phyla (plural of phylum). Life on the earth is divided into five kingdoms: Animalia (animals), Plantae (plants), Fungi, Protista (protozoans and eucaryotic algae), and Monera (blue-green algae).

K-T BOUNDARY

The K-T Boundary was the boundary between the Cretaceous and Tertiary periods, occurring 65 million years ago. This was a time of the huge K-T mass extinction.

K-T EXTINCTION

The K-T extinction was the mass extinction that occurred 65 million years ago, at the boundary of the Cretaceous and Tertiary periods.

KUDZU

Kudzu is a type of legume, a flowering plant that bears its protein-rich seeds in pods and can fix nitrogen from the soil (due to the symbiotic root bacteria rhizobia). Its tubers are edible and the fiber is useful. The plant has a woody stem, wide leaves, and purple flowers. Kudzu is native to Japan and was introduced to the United States around 1876; it soon became a nuisance weed in the southern US. Classification: Kingdom Plantae, class Magnoliopsida, order Rosales, family Leguminosae (pulses), genus Pueraria, specie *P. hunbergiana*.

L

LAGERSTATTEN

Lagerstätten (meaning "fossil deposit places" in German) are geological deposits that are rich with varied, well-preserved fossils, representing a wide variety of life from a particular era. These spectacular fossil deposits represent an amazing "snapshot" in time. Some Lagerstätten include the La Brea Tar Pits (California, USA), Ediacara Hills (South Australia), Burgess Shale (B.C., Canada), Solnhofen (Germany), and Mazon Creek (Illinois, USA),

LAMINA

The lamina is the blade of a leaf.

LANCEOLATE

Lanceolate leaves are shaped like a lance; they have a broad base and taper to a point.

LATERAL

Lateral means of, near, or from the side of an organism.

LATEX

Latex is a milky substance that is tapped from rubber trees.

LAURASIA

Laurasia was the northern supercontinent formed after Pangaea broke up during the Jurassic period. Laurasia included what are now North America, Europe, Asia, Greenland, and Iceland.

LAVA

Lava is molten rock. It usually comes out of erupting volcanoes.

LEAF

A leaf is an outgrowth of a plant that grows from a node in the stem. Most leaves are flat and contain chloroplasts; their main function is to make food energy through photosynthesis. The first leaf to grow from a seed is called the cotyledon.

LEAF ABSCISSION

Leaf abscission is the normal separation of a leaf from a plant. Abscisic acid is the plant hormone involved in leaf abscission.

LEAF AXIL

The leaf axil is where the petiole of the leaf attaches to the stem.

LEAF DIMORPHISM

Having two types of leaves on the same plant.

LEAF GAP

A leaf gap is a break or gap in the plant's stele (cylinder of vascular tissue) at the base of a node (where a leaf is). In the absence of a leaf, there would be no gap, i.e., an unbroken cylinder of vascular tissue

LEAFLET

A leaflet is part of a compound leaf. Each leaflet looks like a small leaf.

LEAF SCAR

A leaf scar is mark on a plant's stem that is left where a leaf was once attached.

LEGUME

A legume is a flowering plant that bears its protein-rich seeds in pods and can fix nitrogen from the soil (due to the symbiotic root bacteria, rhizobia). Some legumes include lentils, beans, clover, alfalfa, lespedezas, vetches, kudzu, and peas. Classification: Kingdom Plantae, class Magnoliopsida, order Rosales, family Leguminosae.

LEMMA

A lemma is a bract (a reduced, leaf-like structure associated with a flower) in a grass spikelet that is located below the stamens and pistil of the flower.

LENTICEL

A lenticel is a small pore in the bark of a tree through which gas exchange occurs.

LEPIDODENDRON

Lepidodendron (also known as the "scale tree") was a giant club moss (a tree-like plant) whose long trunk had bark with a diamond-shaped pattern (the scars of old, dead branches that fell off). This ancient lycopod was over 130 ft (40 m) tall; the trunk was over 6 ft (1.8 m) in diameter. Lepidodendron lived in swampy areas during the Carboniferous Period (about 360 to 286 million years ago). It has spirally-arranged leaves that ended in cones. By the time the dinosaurs lived, the giant club mosses had died out and were replaced by smaller club mosses.

LEPTOCYCAS

Leptocycas gracilis was a cycad (a primitive seed plant) that lived during the late Triassic period. It was a palm-like tree with a long, woody trunk that lived in warm climates. This tree was about 4.8 ft (1.5 m) tall. Separate male and female plants exist (they are dioecious). This gymnosperm had long, divided leaves and produced large seed cones.

LIANA

Liana is a woody, climbing vine that grows on tree trunks in order to reach sunlight in the rainforest. Rattan, used for making wicker furniture, is made from liana vines.

LIAS EPOCH

The Lias epoch was the early part of the Jurassic period, about 206 to 180 million years ago.

LICHEN

Lichens are organisms that are a symbiosis between algae and fungus. The photosynthetic algae produces food and the fungus provides protection for the algae. Lichens can survive in a variety of conditions and are found worldwide.

LIGNOTUBER

A lignotuber is a root or woody stem base that stores water.

LIGNULE

Lignules (which means tongue) are the two small flaps at the base of a monocot's leaf that wrap around the stem.

LIPID

A lipid is a fat. Membranes in cells are composed of two lipid layers (with proteins dissolved within them).

LINNEAN SYSTEM

The linnean system is a method of classifying organisms based on a simple hierarchical structure. Organisms are divided into groups using the following system: Kingdom, Phylum, Class, Order, Family, Genus and Species.

LIVERWORT

Liverwort is a green, moss-like plant belonging to the family Hepaticae. This small, simple plant lives in moist, shady areas and has wide, flat leaves that lie close to the ground. Liverworts reproduce with spores.

LIVING FOSSILS

Living fossils are organisms that lived during ancient times and still live today, like the Coelacanth, the horseshoe crab, the gingko tree, cycads, horsetails, club mosses, and many, many other well-adapted organisms.

LOAM

Loam is a type of rich, crumbly soil that contains an almost equal amount of sand and silt, plus a smaller amount of clay (it contains from 28 to 50% silt, less than 52% sand, and 7 to 27% clay).

LOBED

A lobed leaf is one in which the margin is divided into rounded or pointed sections and the incisions (cuts) go less than halfway to the midrib.

LOESS

Loess is the term for soil particles that have been moved to another location by the wind.

LONGITUDINAL STRIATE VENATION

Longitudinal striate venation is a vein pattern found in monocots leaves. A leaf with longitudinal striate venation has its veins arranged almost parallel to one another, running the length of the leaf (also called parallel venation).

LOW SEASONALITY

Low seasonality is when there is a small difference in temperature between the seasons (with mild winters and summers).

LYCOPSIDS

Lycopsids (club mosses) are primitive, vascular plants (pteridophytes) that evolved over 375 million years ago (during the Devonian). Huge club mosses went extinct during the Permian mass extinction; smaller ones lived during the time of the dinosaurs. These plants live near moisture (in order for their spores to germinate). These fast-growing, resilient plants propagate with rhizomes (underground stems).

LYSOSOME

Lysosomes are organelles within plant cells (and other eukaryotic cells) that contain digestive enzymes and is involved with the digestion of food. A lysosome fuses with a vacular membrane that contains food, and the lysosome's enzymes digest the food, breaking the food down into its components.

M

MAASTRICHTIAN AGE

The Maastrichtian age was the last part of the Cretaceous period, about 71 to 65 million years ago, at the very end of the Mesozoic era.

MAGNETIC FIELD

The earth's magnetic field is aligned with the north and south poles, and has reversed many times during geologic history. A fossil's magnetic orientation can give clues to its date.

MALM EPOCH

The Malm epoch was the late (or upper) part of the Jurassic period, about 159 to 144 million years ago.

MANGROVE

Mangroves are tropical evergreen trees and shrubs. They live near the shore in tropical marshes and tidal shores with their adventitious roots in the salt water. Classification: genus Rhizophora. Some mangroves include the red mangrove (*Rizophora mangle*), the black mangrove (*Avicennia germinans*), and the white mangrove (*Laguncularia racemosa*).

MANGROVE FOREST

A mangrove forest (also called a mangrove swamp) is an expanse of mangrove trees. These trees live near the shore in tropical marshes and tidal shores with their adventitious roots in the salt water..

MARGINS

The margins of a leaf are its edges, which very from plant to plant. The margins can be smooth, serrated, or toothed; they can also be lobed or entire.

MASSARANDUBA TREE

The Massaranduba tree (*Manilkara bidentata*)), also called the cow tree, macaranduba, bulletwood, and balata, is a large rainforest tree whose sap is milky white and is edible. Its fruit is also edible. This tree grows to about 100 to 150 feet tall and has a diameter of 2 to 6 feet. The tree's unusual bark is deeply-scored, reddish and ragged. The bark is used to produce a red dye. Many Massaranduba trees are in the rainforest are being harvested for its durable lumber.

MASS EXTINCTION

Mass extinction is the process in which huge numbers of species die out suddenly. The dinosaurs (and many other species) went extinct during the K-T extinction, probably because of an asteroid that hit the earth.

MEDULLARY RAYS

Medullary rays (also called wood rays) are bundles of cells that radiate from the center of a tree like the spokes of a wheel (they are most easily seen in the cross section of a tree trunk). They store food and transport it horizontally within the tree.

MEIOSIS

Meiosis is a process in which an eukaryotic cell's (diploid) nucleus divides twice and produces four daughter cells (called gametes or reproductive cells), each of which have half the genetic complement of the parent cell (they are haploid). This process was named by Farmer and Moore in 1905.

MERISTEM

The meristem is a group of plant cells that can divide indefinitely. The meristem provides new cells for the plant.

MESIC

Mesic environmental conditions are ones with medium moisture (water).

MESIC SOIL

Mesic soil is a medium type of soil (hence the name, which means middle) that drains well yet retains some water. Mesic soil is exellent for farming.

MESOPHYLL

Mesophyll is the internal tissue of a photosynthetic leaf.

MESOPHYTE

A mesophyte is a plant that has moderate water requirements.

MESOZOIC ERA

The Mesozoic Era ("The Age of Reptiles"), occurred from 248-65 million years ago. It is divided into the Triassic, Jurassic, and Cretaceous periods. Dinosaurs, mammals, and flowering plants evolved during the Mesozoic, and Pangaea broke up. The era ended with the K-T mass extinction.

METAMORPHIC ROCK

Metamorphic rocks are compacted by pressure and heat from deep inside the earth.

METEOR

A meteor is a meteoroid that has entered the earth's atmosphere, usually making a fiery trail as it falls. It is sometimes called a shooting star. Most burn up before hitting the earth.

METEORITE

A meteorite is a meteor that has fallen to earth. Meteorites are either stone, iron, or stony-iron.

METEOROID

Meteoroids are tiny stones or pieces of metal that travel through space.

MICROPYLE

The micropyle is the small pore in a seed that that allows water absorption.

MIDRIB

The midrib (rachis) is the central rib of a leaf. It is usually continuous with the petiole and is often raised above the lamina (the leaf blade). On a compound leaf, the midrib extends from the first set of leaflets (where the petiole ends) to the end of the leaf.

MILANKOVITCH THEORY

The Milankovitch theory attempts to explain major temperatures changes on the earth, especially ice ages, by slight variations in the amount of sunlight reaching the earth caused by the eccentricity of the earth's orbit around the Sun. The earth's orbital eccentricity changes the earth's average distance from the sun and therefore slightly changes the amount of sunlight reaching the earth. Milankovitch looked over the past 600,000 years and correlated summer temperature mimnima with four major ice ages in this time. Eccentricity cycles last over 100,000 years. This theory was proposed by Milutin Milankovitch in 1938. Recently, scientists (Richard A. Muller and Gordon J. MacDonald, July 11, 1997, *Science*) have found that changes in the axal tilt of the earth's orbit more closely match glacial cycles for the past million years.

MILDEW

Mildew is a parasitic, filamentous fungus that grows on a host plant.

MILKWEED

Milkweed (genus Asclepius) is a common plant that contains toxins (poisons). There are more than 100 species of this perennial herb, containing varying concentrations of toxic chemicals (glycosides). Monarch butterflies (and other milkweed butterflies) lay their eggs on milkweed leaves; the caterpillars eat milkweed leaves to incorporate the milkweed toxins into their bodies in order to poison their predators.

MILKWEED BUTTERFLIES

Milkweed butterflies are members of the family Danaidae. As larva, they eat the milkweed plant. Milkweed butterflies include the Monarch (*Danaus plexippus*), the Queen (*Danaus gilippus*), and others.

MILLION

A million is a thousand thousand. The dinosaurs lived millions of years ago.

MINERAL

A mineral is a naturally-occurring solid of definite chemical composition whose atoms usually form a regular pattern.

MITOCHONDRION

Mitochondria (the plural of mitochondrion) are organelles within most eukaryotic cells - they power cells by generating energy (in the form of ATP, adenosine triphosphate) by breaking down glucose (a type of sugar). Mitochondria are self-replicating and bound by membranes.

MITOSIS

Mitosis is a process in which an eukaryotic cell's nucleus divides after having duplicated its chromosomes—it produces two daughter cells that are genetically identical to the parent cell and to each other. Walter Flemming (1843-1905), discovered and named this process in 1870.

MIXED WOODLAND

A mixed woodland is a woodland that has both conifers and broadleaf trees.

MOLD

Mold is a type of fungus (and not a plant). Like other fungi, molds do not contain any chlorophyll (and cannot make their own food); molds live off the food produced by plants or animals, or decaying matter. Molds are often parasites on plants, animals, or even other fungi. Molds reproduce with spores. Some molds spoil our food, but other foods are produced by the action of mold (for example, blue, Roquefort, and Camembert chesses have mold growing in them, giving them their flavor). The anti-bacterial drug penicillin is made from the Penicillium mold (Alexander Fleming discovered penicillin in 1928). Classification: Kingdom Fungi, Division Eumycota (septate fungi), Classes Hyphomycetes, Oomycetes, and Zygomycetes.

MONERA

Monera is a prokaryotic kingdom (separate from the plant kingdom) that includes the earliest forms of life on the earth, like archaebacteria (the oldest types of bacteria), eubacteria (like *E. coli*), and cyanobacteria (blue-green bacteria).

MONOCOT

A monocot is a type of flowering plant (an angiosperm) whose seed has one embryonic leaf (cotyledon). The leaves of monocots generally have parallel venation (the veins are parallel to one another). The roots of monocots are usually fibrous and the flower parts are often in multiples of three.

MONOCULTURE

Monoculture is a system of agriculture in which a single type of crop is grown in an area.

MONOECIOUS

Monoecious plants have the male and female reproductive organs on the same plant.

MONOPHYLETIC

A monophyletic group consists of all organisms that share a particular common ancestor (and therefore have similar features). The members of a monophyletic group are more closely related to one other than they are to any organism outside the group. A monophyletic group is also called a clade. An example of a monophyletic group is mammals.

MONOPODIAL

Monopodial (meaning "one foot") is a type of plant growth in which the plant has a single main stem.

MORPHOLOGY

Morphology is the study of the external structure of organisms. For example, the arrangement of leaves on a plant.

MORRISON FORMATION

The Morrison Formation is a rock outcropping located in Utah, USA. This exposed sedimentary rock dates from the late Jurassic period, when this area was similar to a savanna (without the grass, since flowering plants hadn't evolved yet). Dinosaurs like Allosaurus, Seismosaurus, Ceratosaurus, Ornitholestes, and Diplodocus have been found at the Morrison foundation.

MOSS

Moss is a small, low-growing, green plant that has a stem, leaves, and rhizomes, but no vascular system. Mosses reproduce with spores or by forming gametes. Classification: Kingdom Plantae (plants), Plylum Bryophyta (mosses), Four Classes: Class Sphagnopsida (Peat Mosses), Class Takakiopsida ("Takakiophytes"), Class Andreaeopsida (Granite Mosses), Class: Bryopsida or Musci ("True" Mosses). The true mosses (Class Bryopsida/Musci) are divided into three subclasses: Subclass Polytrichidae, Subclass Tetraphidae, Subclass Bryidae.

MUCIGEL

Mucigel is a slimy, protective substance that is secreted by plant roots.

MULTICELLULAR

Multicellular organisms consist of many cells.

MUSHROOM

Mushrooms are fast-growing fungi (they are not plants). They grow in dark, damp places and reproduce via spores.

MUTUALISM

Mutualism is an association between two different species of organisms in which both benefit from the association.

An example of mutualism is the relationship between bees and the flowers they sip nectar from- the bees get nectar from the flower and the flower gets pollinated by the bees. Mutualism used to be called symbiosis, which is now a more general term.

MYA

"mya" stands for millions of years ago.

MYCORRHIZAE

Mycorrhizae is a fungus that grows in a symbiotic relationship with the roots (or rhizoids) of a plant.

N

NANOFOSSIL

Nanofossils are microscopic fossils that are very abundant, widely distributed, and time-specific (because of their high evolutionary rates). They are very useful index fossils.

NATURAL SELECTION

Natural selection is the process in which some organisms live and reproduce and others die before reproducing. Some life forms survive and reproduce because they are better suited to environmental pressures, ensuring that their genes are perpetuated in the gene pool.

NATURALIST

A naturalist is a person who studies plants and animals.

NECTAR

Nectar is the sweet liquid produced by many flowers. Nectar attracts many insects (like butterflies and bees) who go from flower to flower sipping nectar, causing the pollination of the flowers.

NEEDLE

A needle is a long, thin, pointed, needle-shaped leaf, like that of the pine. The word acicular is sometimes used to describe needles.

NEOCOMIAN EPOCH

The Neocomian epoch was the early (lower) part of the Cretaceous period, about 144 to 127 million years ago.

NEOGENE

The Neogene (24 million to 1.8 million years ago) was the later part of the Tertiary Period. It is divided into the Miocene Epoch (24 million to 5 million years ago, when many mammals appeared, including the horses, dogs, bears, South American monkeys, apes in southern Europe, and Ramapithecus; also, modern birds appear) and the Pliocene Epoch (5 million to 1.8 million years ago, when the first hominids (australopithecines) developed, modern forms of whales appeared, and Megalodon swam the seas).

NEOTROPICAL

The neotropical region extends from the southern tip of South America up to Mexico. This vast region includes many different habitats, including tropical rainforests.

NICHE

A niche is a place or position that an organism occupies in an environment.

NITROGEN FIXING

Some bacteria (rhizobia) are nitrogen-fixing; they transform nitrogen gas in the atmopshere into a form that can be used by plants.

NODE

A node is a part of the stem of a plant from which a leaf, branch, or aerial root grows.

NODULE

A nodule is a small, rounded knot on some leguminous plant roots which contain nitrogen-fixing bacteria (rhizobia). For example, peanut plant roots have nodules.

NOXIOUS WEED

A noxious weed is a plant that is considered by local authorities to be a problem, growing where it is not wanted.

NUCLEAR ENVELOPE

The nuclear envelope is double membrane that surrounds the nucleus.

NUCLEUS

The nucleus is a membrane-bound organelle in each plant cell which contains the genetic material of the cell (DNA in chromosomes). It is where DNA (deoxyribonucleic acid) replicates itself, and where RNA (ribonucleic acid) is made. The plural of nucleus is nuclei.

NUCLEOLUS

The nucleolus is a spherical or ovoid organelle in the nucleus of a eukaryotic cell. It consists of granules of DNA and RNA, and synthesizes ribosomal RNA. The plural of nucleolus is nucleoli.

NURSE LOG

A nurse log is a fallen tree trunk that nourishes new life on the forest floor as it decomposes. It provides a rich, moist habitat for ferns, lichens, mosses, and tree seedlings.

NUTRIENT

A nutrient is a chemical that an organism need to ingest in order to survive (like fats, carbohydrates, vitamins, minerals, etc.).

NUCLEAR MEMBRANE

Also called the nuclear envelope. The nuclear membrane is double membrane that surrounds the nucleus of the cell.

O

OMNIVORE

Omnivores are animals that eat both animals and plants.

ORDER

In Linnean classification, an order is a group of related or similar organisms. An order contains one or more families. A group of similar orders forms a class.

ORDOVICIAN PERIOD

The Ordovician period lasted from 505 to 438 million years ago. Primitive plants appear on land, as do the first corals, primitive fishes, seaweed and fungi. Graptolites, bryozoans, gastropods, bivalves, and echinoids also appear. There were high sea levels at first, then global cooling and glaciation, and extensive volcanism. North America was under shallow seas. The Ordovician ended in huge extinction, probably due to glaciation. The Ordovician was named for an ancient tribe (the Ordovices) that lived in northern Wales.

ORGAN

An organ is a specialized tissue (a group of cells) in multicellular organisms that performs a particular function. For example, the ovary is an organ that produces ovules.

ORGANELLE

An organelle is membrane-bound structure within a plant's cell (and all eukaryotic cells) where specialized metabolic tasks occur. Some organelles include the nucleus, nucleolus, mitochondria, the ER (endoplamic reticulum), and lysosomes.

OSMOSIS

Osmosis is a process in which water moves across a semi-permeable membrane in order to equalize the concentration of the solution on both sides. For example, water will move across a cell membrane from areas of low salinity (a hypotonic solution) to areas of high salinity (a hypertonic solution) to equalize the concentrations (and create two isotonic solutions).

OSMOTIC PRESSURE

Osmotic pressure is a phenomenon in which water exerts pressure against a membrane (when it is bordered by solutions of differing concentrations).

OSMOTIC POTENTIAL

Osmotic potential is the potential of water to move into a region by the process of osmosis, the potential of the water to travel from a hypotonic (low concentration) solution to a hypertonic (high concentration) solution.

OUTCROPPING

An outcropping is a place where the bedrock (the underlying rock) is exposed on the earth's surface.

OVARY

An ovary is a female reproductive organ in plants that produces ovules.

OVERBURDEN

The overburden is the rock that lies on top of a fossil.

OVULE

An ovule is the female reproductive cell of flowering plants and cone-bearing plants. After the ovule is fertilized by the male pollen, the ovule becomes a seed.

P

PALEOBOTANY

Palcobotany is the branch of botany that studies the plants that existed in former geologic periods, chiefly by studying fossils.

PALEONTOLOGIST

A paleontologist is a scientist who studies paleontology, the forms of life that existed in former geologic periods, chiefly by studying fossils.

PALEONTOLOGY

Paleontology is the branch of biology that studies the forms of life that existed in former geologic periods, chiefly by studying fossils. "Paleo" means old or ancient. "Ontology" is the study of existence ("onto-" means existence, "-logy" is the study of something).

PALEOZOIC ERA

The Paleozoic Era (540 to 248 million years ago) saw an explosion of new life forms. The Paleozoic (meaning "ancient life") ended with the largest mass extinction in geologic history and was followed by the Mesozoic Era. It is divided into the Cambrian, Ordovician, Silurian, Devonian, Carboniferous, and Permian periods. It was followed by the Mesozoic Era, the time of the dinosaurs.

PALISADE PARENCHYMA

The palisade parenchyma (also called the palisade layer) is a layer of tightly-packed, tube-shaped, chlorophyll-containing cells (chlorenchyma) that is the major photosynthetic layer of a leaf. The palisade layer is located in the upper mesophyll of a leaf (just beneath the upper dermal layer of the leaf).

PALM

A palm is an evergreen tree and a monocot. Classification: Division Magnoliophyta (Angioperms), Class Liliopsida (Monocots), Subclass Arecidae, Order Arecales, Family Arecaceae (or Palmae) (Palms).

PALMATE

A palmate leaf has a hand-like structure. It has more than three lobes that branch from a single point at the base of the leaf.

PALMATE VENATION

A leaf with palmate venation has the main veins arising from a point at the base of the leaf.

PANGAEA

Pangaea was a supercontinent consisting of all of earth's land masses. It existed during the Permian through the Jurassic period. It began breaking up during the Jurassic, forming the continents Gondwanaland and Laurasia.

PANTHALASSA

Panthalassa (meaning "All seas") was the super-ocean that existed on the earth during the time of the super-continent Pangaea. Panthalassa existed during the Permian through the Jurassic period, when Pangaea began to break up; the Tethys sea formed between the northern and southern parts of pangaea as they drifted apart.

PARAPHYLETIC

A paraphyletic group (also called a grade) consists of a common ancestor and some, but not all, of its descendants. These are incomplete groups based primarily on physical characteristics rather than directly on evolutionary relationships. An example of a paraphyletic group is the dinosaurs (without including the birds).

PARALLEL VENATION

A leaf with parallel venation (also called longitudinal-striate venation) has its veins arranged almost parallel to one another.

PARASITE

A parasite is an organism which uses its host for food and/ or shelter. A parasite gives its host nothing in return, and often makes it sick or even kills the host. Termites are a parasite of many trees.

PARASITISM

Parasitism is arelationship between two organisms in which one organism benefits at the other organism's expense. Lice are an example of a parasite that affects many animals; termites are a parasite that are destructive to many trees. Parasitism is a type of symbiosis.

PARENCHYMA

Parenchyma are generalized (undifferentiated) cell or tissue in a plant. Parenchyma cells make or store food; they can often divide or differentiate into different types of cells and have thin cell walls. Parenchyma is the most common type of plant cell. The pith is parenchyma cells at the center of the primary stem of a dicot.

PARSIMONY

Parsimony is the scientific idea that the simplest explanation of a phenomenon is the best one.

PARTED

A parted (also called cleft) leaf is one in which the margins between the irregular teeth go more than halfway to the midrib.

PEANUT PLANT

The peanut plant (*Arachis hypogea*) is a legume that is native to South America (it now grows around the world). The peanut plant grow to about about 60 cm tall and has yellow flowers (1-2 cm long). The flower blooms for about half a day. About 4 days later, a stem (also called a peg) will grow from the flower and head into the soil. At the end of each stem, the seed pods (peanuts in the shell) will grow. The peanut is an annual plant (it completes its life cycle in one year).

PEAT

Peat is a type of soil that is composed of incompletely decomposed plant material that water-logged and low in oxygen.

PEDICEL

A pedicel is plant stalk that attaches a single flower or fruit to the main branch of the inflorescence.

PEDOGENESIS

Pedogenesis is the natural process in which soil forms.

PEDUNCLE

A peduncle is plant stalk that bears an inflorescence or single flower.

PENNSYLVANIAN PERIOD

The Pennsylvanian Period lasted from 325 to 280 million years ago. During this time, the first reptiles (like Hylonomus) appeared and ferns dominated the warm, swampy landscape.

PERENNATE

A plant that perennates lives from year to year (it is a perennial).

PERENNIAL

A perennial plant has a life cycle that lives for more than two years. Perennials usually flower each year.

PERFECT FLOWER

A perfect flower has both male (stamen) and female (ovary) reproductive organs on the same flower.

PERIANTH

The perianth (which means "around the anthers") is the sepals and petals of a flower.

PERICARP

The pericarp is the fruit wall that develops from the ovary wall. The pericarp is divided into the endocarp, mesocarp and exocarp.

PERICARPAL

The pericarpal is the upper part of the flower stem, the receptable, and the lower part of the pistil.

PERIOD

The period is the basic unit of geological time in which a single type of rock system is formed, lasting tens of millions of years.

PERMIAN EXTINCTION

The Permian extinction was the largest mass extinction that ever occurred on the earth, but its causes are unknown. It occurred at end of the Permian period, about 248 million years ago. It in, trilobites went extinct, as did 50% of all animal families, 95% of all marine species, and many trees. Groups that went extinct included: the fusulinid foraminifera, trilobites, rugose and tabulate corals, blastoids, acanthodians, placoderms, and pelycosaurs (like Dimetrodon). Groups that were substantially affected included: bryozoans, brachiopods, ammonoids, sharks, bony fish, crinoids, eurypterids, ostracodes, and echinoderms. This extinction was followed by the Triassic period of the Mesozoic Era.

PERMIAN PERIOD

The Permian period (named after the Perm Province in northeast Russia where rocks from this period were first described) is known as "The Age of Amphibians" (280 to 248 million years ago), this is when Pangaea formed and earth's atmosphere was oxygenated to modern levels. In the early Pemian, labyrinthodonts dominated the land. The Permian ended with the largest mass extinction and was followed by the Mesozoic Era.

PERMINERALIZATION

Permineralization is the process in which minerals are deposited into a bony fossil.

PETAL

A petal is one of the leafy structures that comprise a flower. Petals are often brightly-colored and have many different shapes. They are located between the sepals and the flower's reproductive organs.

PETIOLATE

Petiolate means having a petiole.

PETIOLE

A petiole is a leaf stalk. On a compound leaf, the petiole extends from the stem to the first set of leaflets. A leaf without a petiole is sessile.

PETRIFICATION

Petrification is the process in which an organic tissue turns to stone. The original materials are repaced by minerals.

PETRIFIED WOOD

Petrified wood is fossilized wood. Minerals seeped into buried logs, replacing the original tissues with rock.

PHANEROZOIC EON

The Phanerozoic (meaning "visible life") is the time in which life forms with skeletons or hard shells existed. It is the period from about 540 million years ago until the present.

PHENETICS

Phenetics is a method of attempting to classify biological organisms that does not use genetic or evolutionary information; it was invented by Sokal and Sneath in 1963. In a phenogram, organisms are grouped by superficial overall similarity. Phenetics was abandoned by most scientists in the 1980's because its classifications were arbitrary, mostly useless, and unstable. Paul Ehrlich was a proponent of this system.

PHLOEM

Phloem is plant tissue that conducts nutrients (food) through the plant. In woody-stemmed plants, the phloem is the inner layer of the bark.

PHOMA

Phoma is a genus of fungus that lives on a wide variety of plants (including sunflower, cabbage, banana, etc.). Phoma is characterized by large, black lesions on the stem and/or leaves of the infected plant. About 80 species of phoma have been described.

PHOTOSYNTHESIS

Photosynthesis is the process in which plants convert sunlight, water, and carbon dioxide into food (sugars and starches), oxygen and water. Chlorophyll or closely-related pigments (substances that color the plant) are essential to the photosynthetic process.

PHOTOTROPISM

Phototropism is the bending of a plant in response to sunlight. This reaction is caused by the growth hormone auxin that is contained in the stem.

PHYLLOCLADE

A phylloclade is a flattened stem that looks like a leaf.

PHYLLODE

A phyllode is a leaf that has an enlarged midrib and no blades.

PHYLOGENY

Phylogeny is the evolutionary relationship between organisms. The phylogeny of an organism reflects the evolutionary branch that led up to the organism.

PHYLUM

(plural plyla) In classification, a phylum is a group of related or similar organisms. A phylum contains one or more classes. A group of similar phyla forms a Kingdom. The plant phyla include: Ginkgophyta, Lycophyta (lower ferns like clubmosses), Pterophyta (ferns), Psilophyta (whisk ferns), Anthophyta (flowering plants), Gnetophyta, Sphenophyta, Coniferophyta (conifers), Cycadophyta (cycads), Sphenophyta, and Bryophyta (mosses, liverworts, hornworts).

PINNATE COMPOUND LEAF

A pinnate compound leaf is made up of many small leaflets arranged in pairs on either side of a long central midrib (the rachis). There is often a single terminal leaflet at the end of the midrib.

PINNATELY LOBED LEAF

Pinnately lobed leaves have many lobes arranged along the midrib.

PINNATE VENATION

A leaf with pinnate venation has its veins arranged in pairs coming from a main central midrib vein (the rachis).

PIONEER

A pioneer is a plant that is the first (or among the first) to live in a new area.

PISTIL

The pistil is the central set of female reproductive organs in a flower. The pistil is composed of one or more carpels and produces the ovule.

PISTILLATE

Pistillate flowers have a pistil or pistils.

PITH

The pith is parenchyma cells at the center of the primary stem of a dicot.

PLANT

A plant is a member of the kingdom Plantae, a living organism that undergoes photosynthesis.

PLANT SUCCESSION

Plant succession is the natural pattern of ecosystem growth and change over time for a particular environment. Plant life follows established patterns of growth and change after major distruptions, like fires, floods, agricultural damage, logging, etc. Generally, smaller, fast-growing herbaceous species and grasses grow first in an open field, followed in a few years by softwood tree seedlings and larger herbaceous species. As a young forest develops into a mature forest (30 to 70 years), an understory of smaller hardwood trees develops. The final stage is a climax hardwood forest (100 plus years).

PLANTAE

Plantae is a kingdom in the classificaton of life on the earth. Plantae (plants) is divided into non-vascular plants, vascular plants, and seed plants.

PLASMA MEMBRANE

A plasma membrane (also called the cell membrane or plasmalemma) surrounds each cell and separates it from the environment. In pants, the cell membrane contains cellulose (a carbohydrate).

PLASMALEMMA

A plasmalemma (also called the cell membrane or plasma membrane) surrounds each cell and separates it from the environment. In pants, the cell membrane contains cellulose (a carbohydrate).

PLASMID

A plasmid is a circular loop of DNA found in prokaryotic cells (like those of bacteria). Eukaryotic cells prokaryotic cells (like plant and animal cells) do not have plasmids, they have chromosomes.

PLATE TECTONICS

Plate tectonics is the new-established theory that chunks of the earth's crust (plates) float on the surface and change both position and size over time.

PLATYSPERMS

Platysperms (meaning "flat seeds") are plants with flattened ovules. Platysperms include gingkos, conifers, glossopterids, and cordaites.

PLEISTOCENE

The Pleistocene was an epoch of geologic time that lasted from 1.8 million to 11,000 years ago; it was a period of widespread glaciation and large Ice Age animals (caled Pleistocene Megafauna). The first humans (Homo sapiens) evolved during the Pleistocene. Mammoths, mastodons, saber-toothed cats, giant ground sloths, and other Ice Age mammals evolved. A mass extinction of large mammals and many birds occurred about 10,000 years ago, probably caused by Ice Ages.

PLESIOMORPHY

Plesiomorphy (meaning "old form") is a primitive character of a group.

PLUMULE

The plumule is the shoot of a plant embryo (in the seed before germination).

PNEUMATOPHORE

A pneumatophore is an air-transporting vessel in plants.

POD

A seed pod is an elongated, two-sided vessel that contain several fertilized seeds. It is a dehiscent fruit or pedicarp - the pod splits open when the seeds are mature. Beans and peas are some plants that have pods.

PODZOL

Podzol is a kind of soil that is very low in humus.

POLLEN

Pollen is the male reproductive cell of flowering plants and cone-bearing plants. Pollen grains are produced in the anther of a flower.

POLLEN TUBE

After the male's pollen grains have landed on the stigma during fertilization, pollen tubes develop within the style. The pollen tubes transport the sperm from the grain to the ovum (where fertilization of the egg occurs and the seeds will develop).

POLLENATION

Pollination is the transfer of pollen from the anther to the stigma.

POLLINATION

Pollination is the process in which the male's pollen fertilizes the female's ovule and creates a seed; the pollen is transferred from the male's anther to the female's stigma. Pollination is effected by the wind, insects, hummingbirds, etc.

POLLINIUM

A pollinium (or pollinia) is a mass of fused pollen grains that is produces by a single anther. This mass sticks together and during pollination is transported as a single unit. Orchids have polliniums.

POLYPHYLETIC

A polyphyletic group consists of organisms but not their common ancestors. This is an artificial group which is based primarily on physical characteristics rather than on evolutionary relationships. An example is "flying vertebrates" which includes birds, pteranodons and bats.

PRECAMBRIAN

The Precambrian is the time 540 before the Cambrian period (before million years ago). It is the time from when the earth formed until simple life-forms evolved.

PREHISTORIC

Prehistoric refers to the time before people began recording history in writing. This time varies from culture to culture.

PREY

An animal becomes prey when another animal hunts and kills it for food. Insects are the prey of the Venus fly trap.

PRICKLE

A prickle is a a sharp outgrowth of a plant's epidermis (outer skin). Prickles are easily broken off a plant. Roses have prickles.

PRICKLY PEAR CACTUS

Prickly pear cacti (genus Opuntia, many species) are North American desert succulents that have flat, fleshy, leaf-shaped pads and large spines (modified leaves) growing from tubercles (small bumps on the pads). They have red, yellow, or purple flowers. Prickly pear cacti and their fruit are edible.

PRIMARY CONSUMER

A primary consumer is an herbivore (a plant-eater). Primary consumers occupy the second trophic level in the grazing food chain.

PRIMARY FOREST

A primary forest is a forest that has never been logged or disturbed.

PRIMARY GROWTH

Primary growth is plant growth that occurs at the tips (terminal bud) of the stem or the tip of the roots, at the apical meristems. In seed plants, primary growth produces.

PRIMARY ROOT

The primary root is the first root of a plant to develop in the germinating seed. The primary root develops from the radicle of the embryo. It is also called the taproot

PRIMARY VEGETATION

Primary vegetation is the plants life that has been in place since the area reached its climax state.

PRODUCER

A producer (or aurotroph) is an organism that makes its own food from light energy (using photosynthesis), or chemical energy (using chemosynthesis). Most green plants, many protists (one-celled organisms like slime molds) and most bacteria are producers. Producers are the base of the food chain.

PROTOPLAST

A protoplast is a plant or bacterial cell whose cell wall has been removed.

PROTOZOA

Protozoans (meaning "first animals") are a phylum of primitive animals that include the following classes: Mastigophora (flagellates), Sarcodina (amoebas), Sporozoa (Parasites), and Ciliata (Ciliates).

PSAMMOPHILE

A psammophile (meaning "sand loving") is a plant that lives in sand or sandy soils. Some psammophytic plants include *Salix psammophila* (a willow), *Dypsis psammophila* (a palm) and *Cocolobo diversifolia* (the pigeon plum).

PSILOPHYTA

Psilophyta are a division of primitive plants that are also called wisk ferns (they are not true ferns). Psilophytes are seedless vascular plants with underground rhizomes. They live in tropical to sub-tropical areas and are terrestrial or epiphytic. There are only 2 genera (Psilotum and Tmesipteri), and only a few living species.

PTERIDOPHYTES

Pteridophytes are a group of primitive vascular plants that include Lycopods (club mosses), Sphenopsids (horsetails, shown left), and ferns (shown, right). These plants reproduce with spores that germinate only in moist areas; they also reproduce using rhizomes (underground stems). Pteridophytes evolved during the Devonian and were mostly low-growing during the Mesozoic Era. These fast-growing, resilient plants were a source of food for plant-eating dinosaurs that lived in moist areas.

PTERIDOSPERMS

Pteridosperms (Seed ferns) were primitive seed plants (not ferns at all) that lived in swampy areas from the Mississipian Epoch through the Mesozoic Era. They had woody stems studded with dried out leaf bases. The tops had fern-like fronds which bore seeds. Some seed ferns include Glossopteris (pictured above), Dicroidium, Caytonia, Denkania, and Lidgettonia.

PTEROPHYTA

Pterophyta (also called Pteridopsida) is a phylum of plants that includes some ferns, ancient vascular plants. There are about 11,000 living species of Pterophytes.

PULSE

A pulse refers to a leguminous plant that produces edible seeds or to the seeds themselves. Some pulses include peas, beands, and lentils.

PUMPKIN

The pumpkin (*Cucurbita pepo*) is an annual vine from the New World.

R

RACHIS

The rachis is the midrib of a leaf. It is usually continuous with the petiole and is often raised above the lamina (the leaf blade). On a compound leaf, the rachis extends from the first set of leaflets (where the petiole ends) to the end of the leaf.

RADIAL SYMMETRY

Radial symmetry is when a basic shape unit is repeated around a central point (for example, most flowers have radial symmetry).

RADICLE

The radicle is the lower part of a embryo's axis. The radicle develops into the primary root.

RADIOISOTOPE DATING

Radioisotope dating of igneous rock layers is used to find out how old the rock is (when the igneous rock formed). One way of dating fossils is by dating bracketing layers of igneous rock.

RAFFLESIA

The Rafflesia flower (*Rafflesia arnoldi*) is the world's largest flower. This giant bloom is found in rainforests of Indonesia. Locally, it is called the "corpse flower." Rafflesia gives off a putrid smell that reminds people of rotting meat (this odor attracts its pollenators, beetles and flies), hence its nickname. Rafflesia's enormous flower is about 3 feet (1 m) across and weighs about 20 pounds (9 kilograms). The flower takes about a year to develop, then it blooms for about a week before dying. The flower has five wide orange petals (with pale dots) surrounding a spiked cup. Rafflesia has no stem, no roots, and no leaves. The flower is supported by fungus-like tissue that lives in another plant - the Tetrastigma vine.

RAINFOREST

Rainforests are very dense, relatively warm, wet forests. They are havens for millions of plants and animals.

RECEPTACLE

The receptacle is the terminal portion of the flower stalk.

REDWOOD

The redwood is the tallest tree, growing up to 370 feet (113 m) tall and living for over a thousand years. One redwood tree in California is 2,200 years old. The roots of this giant conifer are shallow, but spread sideways up to 250 feet (75 meters) from the trunk. The bark is deeply-furrowed, fibrous, thick [up to about 1 foot (30.5 cm) thick] and lacks resin. There are many species of redwood, including the giant coast redwood, *Sequoia sempervirens*.

REGRESSION

Regression is the exposure of continental land as the sea level decreases, usually caused by increasing polar ice and glacier formation. Another causes is the local uplift of the continental land.

RENIFORM

A reniform leaf is kidney-shaped.

REPAND

A repand leaf has a wavy margin.

RESIN

Resin is a substance secreted by some plants. Resin is often aromatic (having a strong odor); it is insoluble in water but will dissolve in alcohol. Fossilized resin is called amber.

RESINIFEROUS

Resiniferous means producing resin.

$C_6H_{12}O_6 + 6O_2 = 6CO_2 + 6H_2O + ATP$

RESPIRATION

Respiration is a process in which energy is generated in cells. In respiration, glucose (a type of sugar) and oxygen are converted into carbon dioxide, water and ATP (adenosine triphosphate). Respiration takes place in the mitochondrion of both plant and animal cells.

RETICULATE VENATION

A leaf with reticulate venation has its veins arranged in a pattern such that larger veins give rise to progressively smaller veins. The end branches of the veins define small areas called aeroles.

RHIZOBIA

Rhizobia are bacteria that live symbiotically with plants (especially legumes), living on the plant's roots. The rhizobia fix nitrogen (from atmospheric nitrogen) for the plant and the rhizobia get energy from the plant.

RHIZOME

A rhizome is a thick, horizontal underground stem (not a root) of a plant, that grows close to the ground. Rhizomes have nodes and scale-like leaves; roots form on the lower surface and new shoots can form at nodes. Ferns, mosses, horsetails, ginger, irises, and some grasses have rhizomes.

RIBOSOME

Ribosomes are small organelles composed of RNA-rich cytoplasmic granules that are sites of protein synthesis.

RIPARIAN FOREST

A riparian forest is situated by a river bank or other body of water.

RNA

RNA (short for ribonucleic acid) is a complex, organic, single-stranded molecule that is found in the nucleus and the cytoplasm of cells. RNA carries DNA's instructions for chemical synthesis (like protein formation) to the cell and guides the formation of these chemicals. There are many types of RNA that have different functions. The major types of RNA are messenger RNA (mRNA, which carries the information for protein synthesis from the chromosomal DNA to the ribosomes), transfer RNA (tRNA, which translates mRNA and bonds with amino acids to correctly form the desired proteins), and ribosomal RNA (rRNA, found in ribosomes).

ROOT

A root is a plant structure that obtains food and water from the soil, stores energy, and provides support for the plant. Most roots grow underground.

ROOT CAP

The root cap is a cap-shaped structure at the ends (tips) of the roots. It covers and protects the apical meristem (the actively growing region) of the root.

ROOT HAIRS

Root hairs are very thin, hair-like roots that are extensions of the root's epidermis. Root hairs have a large surface area and absorb water and minerals for the plant.

ROOT TIP

The root tip is the tip of the root and contains the root cap and the apical meristem (the actively growing region).

ROUGH ENDOPLASMIC RETICULUM

Rough ER is a vast system of interconnected, membranous, infolded and convoluted sacks that are located in the cell's cytoplasm (the ER is continuous with the outer nuclear membrane). Rough ER is covered with ribosomes that give it a rough appearance. Rough ER transport materials through the cell and produces proteins in sacks called cisternae (which are sent to the Golgi body, or inserted into the cell membrane).

RUBBER TREE

Rubber trees are large trees (belonging to the spurge family, family Euphorbiaceae) that live in tropical (warm) areas. These trees are tapped for their latex (from which rubber is made), which is produced in their bark layers (it is not the sap). The Pará rubber tree (*Hevea brasiliensis*) is native to South American rain forests, and grows to be over 100 ft (30 m) tall. In 1876, Henry Wickham brought seeds from the Para rubber tree (taken from the lower Amazon area of Brazil) to London, England. Seedlings were grown in London, and later sent to Ceylon and Singapore. The technique of tapping rubber trees for their latex was developed in southeast Asia (before that, the trees were cut down to extract the rubber). Commercial rubber production now takes place in Malaysia, Thailand, Indonesia, and Sri Lanka (but not significantly in South America).

RUGOSE

Rugose means ridged, rough, or wrinkled.

RUMINANT

A ruminant is an animal that digests its food many times. This food is usually tough plant material like grasses. Ruminants include cows, sheep, antelopes, and camels.

RUNOFF

Runoff is water that drains or flows from the land into streams and rivers, eventually into seas. The water is generally from rain or snowpack melt.

S

SAGUARO CACTUS

The saguaro cactus (*Carnegiea gigantea*) is a large succulent found in the Sonoran desert of North America. This cactus has accordian-like pleats and long spines. Photosynthesis takes place on its green, chlorophyll-containing trunk. The saguaro has a life span of over 200 years and it can grow to over 50 feet tall. This cactus produces white flowers and a deep red (edible) fruit. Each fruit produces about 2,000 reddish-black seeds.

SAMARA

A samara is a one-seeded fruit, winged, indehiscent fruit, like the seed of the maple and elm (which helicopter their way down from the tree). Samara is Latin for elm seed.

SAMAUMA TREE

The Samauma tree (*Eriodendron samauma*), sometimes called the "Queen of the Forest" or the silk-cotton tree, is a large, rainforest tree that grows to be over 50 m tall. It has an unusual lower trunk/roots that come off the main trunk in large, triangular planes. The soft-wood timber of this tree is pinkish-white. Many Samauma trees in the rainforest are being harvested to make inexpensive plywood.

SAP

Sap is a liquid that circulates within the sapwood of woody plants. Sap rises up from the roots. Sap contains water and minerals; in the spring it also contains sugars (and stimulates the growth of the tree).

SAPLING

A sapling is a small, young tree.

SAPROPHYTE

A saprophyte is a plant that obtains nutrition from dead and decaying plant or animal tissue. Most saprophytes do not produce chlorophyll, and therefore need another source of energy. Most fungi and a few flowering plants (like some orchids and Indian pipe) are saprophytic.

SAPWOOD

Sapwood is the outer layer of wood in a tree and contains living cells. Sap circulates within the sapwood of woody plants.

SAW GRASS

Saw grass, *Cladium jamaicense.*, is a plant that thrives in wet, warm, humid areas (swamps like the Florida Everglades). A member of the sedge family, saw grass has long, tough, sharp-toothed leaves.

SCALE-LIKE LEAVES

Scale-like leaves are tiny, green leaves. On junipers, scale-like leaves overlap and cover the twigs.

SCAT

Scat means animal waste or droppings.

SCLERENCHYMA

Sclerenchyma is a supportive and protective tissue found in plants. Sclerenchyma is composed of hard, thick, dry cells.

SCLEROPHYLL FOREST

A sclerophyll forest is one in which the crowns of the trees form a continuous canopy. The word scherophyll means "hard leaf" in Greek. Sclerophyll forests are often found in Australia - Eucalyptus trees often form a sclerophyll forest. There are wet (over 30 m tall) and dry (10-30 tall) sclerophyll forests

SCLEROPHYLLOUS PLANTS

Sclerophyllous plants are small plants that have hard, thickened leaves and have a relatively short distance along the stem between the leaves (short internodes). Sclerophyllous plants are often from dry areas. The word scherophyll means "hard leaf" in Greek.

SCYTHIAN EPOCH

The Scythian epoch was the early (lower) part of the Triassic period, about 248 million to 242 million years ago, the beginning of the Mesozoic Era.

SEA WEED

Seaweed is a type of aquatic plant that obtains its energy via photosynthesis. Seaweed (like kelp) are not true plants. Seaweeds are usually green, brown, or red.

SEASONS

There are four seasons in the year: winter, spring, summer, and fall (also called autumn).

SECONDARY COMPOUND

A secondary compound is a chemical manufactured by a plant that protects it.

SECONDARY FOREST

A secondary forest (also known as a jungle) is a forest whose canopy trees have been logged (cut), causing lush growth on the forest floor.

SECONDARY GROWTH

Secondary growth is plant growth that does not occur at the tips of the stems or the tip of the roots. In seed plants, secondary growth produces bark and wood.

SEDIMENT

Sediment is any material deposited by wind or water, like rocks and sand.

SEDIMENTARY ROCK

Sedimentary rock is rock that has formed from sediment. Most fossils are found in exposed sedimentary rock.

SEED

The seed is the reproductive unit of some plants.

SEED COAT

The seed coat is the outer, protective layer covering the seed. The seed coat is formed from the two integuments in the developing seed.

SEED DISPERSAL

Seeds are dispersed (spread) by many different methods, including floating on the wind (e.g., dandelions), floating in the water (e.g., coconut, sedge), hitching a ride on an animal (e.g., cranesbill), or being eaten (and then expelled) by a seed dispersing animal (e.g., many fruits).

SEED DISPERSER

A seed disperser is an animal that eats seeds (usually contained in fruit) but does not harm the seed. The seed is excreted in the stool, and the seed is spread away from the parent plant. Some seed dispersers include the kereru (a pigeon from New Zealand) and the cassowary (from Australia and New Guinea).

SEED FERNS

Seed ferns (Pteridosperms) were primitive seed plants (not ferns at all) that lived in swampy areas from the Mississipian Epoch through the Mesozoic Era. They had woody stems studded with dried out leaf bases. The tops had fern-like fronds which bore seeds. Some seed ferns include Glossopteris (pictured above), Dicroidium, Caytonia, Denkania, and Lidgettonia.

SEED POD

A seed pod is an elongated, two-sided vessel that contain several fertilized seeds. It is a dehiscent fruit or pedicarp - the pod splits open when the seeds are mature. Beans and peas are some plants that have pods.

SEED PREDATOR

A seed predator is an animal that eats and destroy seeds instead of eating the fruit and leaving the seed or dispersing the seed in the stool. Parrots are seed predators. Seed predators limit the number of viable seeds.

SELF-POLLINATION

Self-pollination is the transfer of pollen from the anther to the stigma of the same flower or another flower on the same plant.

SENONIAN EPOCH

The Senonion epoch was the late (upper) part of the Cretaceous period, about 89 million to 65 million years ago, the end of the Mesozoic Era.

SEPAL

The sepals are small leaves located directly under a flower. They are the outermost part of a flower. Collectively, the sepals are called the calyx.

SERRATED

Serrated leaves have a jagged edge.

SESSILE

A leaf without a petiole (a leaf stalk) is sessile.

SEXUAL DIMORPHISM

Sexual dimorphism is characteristic of having two different forms, one for the males and another for the females of a species.

SHALE

Shale is a type of rock that is formed from clay that has been pressed into thin sheets.

SHIFTING CULTIVATION

Shifting cultivation is a type of farming in which fields are used for a few years, and are then left to grow in a wild state for many years. This allows the soil to recover and become rich and fertile again.

SHOCKED QUARTZ

Shocked quartz is quartz that has undergone deformation due to extreme pressure and heat. It has been found in the layer that marks the K-T boundary, lending credence to the Alvarez impact theory.

SHOOT

A shoot is new growth on part of a plant.

SHRUB LAYER

The shrub layer is the layer of the rainforest above the forest floor but under the canopy.

SIGNOR-LIPPS EFFECT

The Signor-Lipps Effect explains how a fossil record that appears to be a gradual extinction can actually represent a sudden extinction. If many organisms go extinct at the same time, the fossil record wouldn't necessarily represent the rarer species and the more common equally. The rarer species might disappear from the fossil record long before the time of extinction, simply due to chance.

SILT

Silt is fine dirt (soil or sand) that is carried by running water and deposited as sediment.

SILTATION

Siltation is the build-up of silt that is suspended in rivers or other bodies of water.

SILURIAN PERIOD

The Silurian Period lasted from 438 million to 408 million years ago. The first jawed fishes and uniramians (like insects, centipedes and millipedes) appeared during the Silurian (over 400 million years ago). The first vascular plants (plants with water-conducting tissue as compared with non-vascular plants like mosses) appeared on land (Cooksonia is the first known vascular plant). During this time, there were high seas worldwide until the end of the Silurian. Brachiopods, crinoids, corals, and eurypterids (sea scorpions) lived in the seas.

SIMPLE LEAF

A simple leaf is a leaf with only one lamina for each petiole (that is, each leaf blade has one stem).

SIPHONOSTELE

A siphonostele is a type of stele that consists of a cylinder of vascular tissue (xylem and phloem) that surrounds the central pith tissue.

SLASH-AND-BURN FARMING

Slash-and-burn farming is a destructive type of agriculture in which the farmer burns down a new portion of the rainforest every few years in order to cultivate a crop.

SMOOTH ENDOPLASMIC RETICULUM

Smooth ER is a vast system of interconnected, membranous, infolded and convoluted tubes that are located in the cell's cytoplasm (the ER is continuous with the outer nuclear membrane). The space within the ER is called the ER lumen. Smooth ER transport materials through the cell. It contains enzymes and produces and digests lipids (fats) and membrane proteins; smooth ER buds off from rough ER, moving the newly-made proteins and lipids to the Golgi body, lysosomes, and membranes.

SOIL

Soil is a natural, constantly-changing substance that is made up of minerals, organic materials, and living organisms. plants grow in soil.

SOLAR RADIATION

Solar radiation is the heat and light that comes from the sun.

SP.

Sp. is an abbreviation for "species." Sp. is often used when the genus is known, but the species is not.

SPECIATION

Speciation is the process in which a single species differentiates into two distinct species. One method by which this occurs is geographic isolation, in which two subpopulations of a single species are separated and no longer interbreed. Since the pressures of natural selection differ for the two groups, the two populations become more and more different from one other.

SPIKE

A spike is a flower stalk, an ear of grain (such as corn or wheat), or an inflorescence of unstalked flowers.

SPIKELET

A spikelet is a secondary spike found in grasses; it is a cluster of two or more flowers in the inflorescence.

SPINE

A spine is a sharp, modified leaf, scale, or stipule. Cacti have spines.

SPIROGYA

Spirogyra is a genus of multicellular green algae that lives in fresh water. Spirogyra cells are joined end-to-end, forming an unbranched, tube-like structure that contains one or two spirally-wound chloroplasts. Reproduction occurs asexually (as the filament breaks apart forming new strands) and sexually (two filaments meet and merge as the cell walls decay and a protoplast moves from one organism to the other, resulting in a zygote - this occurs under adverse conditions).

SPHENOPSIDS

Sphenopsids (horsetails) are primitive, spore-bearing plant with rhizomes. These fast-growing, resilient plants were common during the Mesozoic Era. The side branches are arranged in rings along the hollow stem. Horsetails date from the Devonian period 408-360 million years ago, but are still around today and are invasive weeds. Huge horsetails went extinct in the Permian mass extinction; smaller ones lived during the Mesozoic Era.

SPONGY MESOPHYLL

Spongy mesophyll is the layer below the palisade mesophyll; it has irregularly-shaped cells with many air spaces between the cells. These cells contain some chlorophyll. The spongy mesophyll cells communicate with the guard cells (stomata), causing them to open or close, depending on the concentration of gases.

SPORE

A spore is a single-celled reproductive unit of some organisms (cryptogams like mushrooms, ferns and mosses). Functionally, a spore is similar to a seed but it does not containan embryo). Spores are usually encapsulated by a rigid wall.

SPROUT

A sprout is a very young plant (newly germinated) or the new growth on a plant (a shoot).

STAMEN

The stamen is the male reproductive parts of a flower. It consists of the filament and the anther, which produces pollen.

STELE

A stele is the central cylinder of vascular bundles in stems and roots.

STEM

A stem is the axis of a plant; it may be above or below the ground.

STIGMA

The stigma is part of the pistil, the female reproductive tissue of a flower. The stigma receives the male pollen grains during fertilization.

STIPE

A stipe is a stem-like structure in some plants, like some kelp and fungi.

STIPULE

Stipules are small, paired appendages (sometimes leaf-life) that are found at the base of the petiole of leaves of many flowering plants.

STOLON

A stolon is an above-ground stem that has buds that sprout to form new shoots, forming a new, genetically-identical plant. Strawberry plants have stolons.

STOMA

A stoma (the plural is stomata) is a pore (or opening) in a plant's leaves. Most of the stoma are on the underside of the leaf. Guard cells open and close the stoma using turgor pressure, controlling the loss of water vapor and other gases from the plant.

STRATA

The strata (singular=stratum) are the different layers of a rainforest. Different animals and plants live in different parts of the rainforest. Scientists divide the rainforest into strata (zones) based on the living environment. Starting at the top, the strata are: emergents, canopy, understory, and forest floor.

STRATIGRAPHY

Stratigraphy is a method of dating fossils by observing how deeply a fossil is buried. Sedimentary rock layers (strata) are formed episodically as earth is deposited horizontally over time. Newer layers are formed on top of older layers, pressurizing them into rocks. Paleontologists can estimate the amount of time that has passed since the stratum containing the fossil was formed. Generally, deeper rocks and fossils are older than fossils found above them.

STRATOCLADISTICS

Stratocladistics is a method of classifying organisms based upon both cladistics (considering common ancestors with shared anatomical characteristics) together with stratiography (information from the fossil record which lets you know which animals lived earlier or later than others; older fossils are deeper than more recent fossils). In stratocladistics, cladograms are generated in which ancestors preceed their descendants.

STRIATE VENATION

Striate venation is a vein pattern found in monocots leaves. A leaf with striate venation has its veins arranged almost parallel to one another.

STROMA

The stroma is part of the chloroplasts in plant cells, located within the inner membrane of chloroplasts, between the grana.

STRONG SEASONALITY

Strong seasonality is when there is a big difference in temperature between the seasons (for example, a hot summer and a cold winter). Compare to low seasonality, in which the difference in temperatures between the seasons is small (with mild winters and summers).

STYLE

The style is part of the pistil, the female reproductive tissue of a flower. The style is a long tube on top of the ovary below the stigma. After the male's pollen grains have landed on the stigma during fertilization, pollen tubes develop within the style. The pollen tubes transport the sperm from the grain to the ovum (where fertilization of the egg occurs and the seeds will develop).

SUCCESSION, PLANT

Plant succession is the natural pattern of ecosystem growth and change over time for a particular environment. Plant life follows established patterns of growth and change after major distruptions, like fires, floods, agricultural damage, logging, etc. Generally, smaller, fast-growing herbaceous species and grasses grow first in an open field, followed in a few years by softwood tree seedlings and larger herbaceous species. As a young forest develops into a mature forest (30 to 70 years), an understory of smaller hardwood trees develops. The final stage is a climax hardwood forest (100 plus years).

SUCCULENT

A succulent is a plant that has fleshy and juicy tissues, like cacti, sedums, aloes, and yuccas.

SUCKER ROOT

A sucker root is a root that emerges from the ground and sends up a shoot which supports the plant.

SUESS, EDUARD

Eduard Suess was an Austrian geologist who first realized that there had once been a land bridge between South America, Africa, India, Australia, and Antarctica. He named this large land mass Gondwanaland (named after a district in India where the fossil plant Glossopteris was found). This was the southern supercontinent formed after Pangaea broke up during the Jurassic period. He based his deductions upon the fossil fern Glossopteris, which is found throughout India, South America, southern Africa, Australia, and Antarctica.

SUSTAINABLE USE

Sustainable use is the judicious use of natural resources without destroying them.

SYMBIOSIS

Symbiosis is a situation in which two dissimilar organisms live together. There are many types of symbiosis, including mutualism (in which both organisms benefit), commensalism (in which one organism benefits and the other is not affected), or parasitism (in which one organism benefits at the other organism's expense). Symbiosis used to be defined as a situation in which two dissimilar organisms live together to the benefit of both - this is now called mutualism. The word symbiosis means "living together"" in Greek.

SYMMETRY

Symmetry across an axis (also called bilateral symmetry) is when one side of an object is the mirror image of its other half - i.e., one half has the same shape and size as the other half (for example, most leaves are bilaterally symmetrical). Radial symmetry is when a basic shape is duplicated around a central point (for example, most flowers have radial symmetry).

SYMPLESIOMORPHY

Symplesiomorphy (meaning "shared old form") is the persistence of ancestral (primitive) traits in different clades.

SYMPODIAL

Sympodial (meaning "with foot") is a type of branching growth in which the terminal bud dies or ends in an inflorescence, and growth (sympodial shoots) continues from lateral buds. What looks like the plant's main axis is actually a series of many lateral branches, each arising from the previous lateral branch. Some bamboos and orchids exhibits sympodial growth.

SYNAPOMORPHY

Synapomorphy (meaning "shared form") is a derived (new) character shared by groups. A synapomorphy can be used to infer common ancestry.

T

TAP ROOT

The tap root is the main root of some plants; the tap root extends straight down under the plant with very little side branches.

TAXON

A taxon is category in the classification of living organisms. The taxa (the plural of taxon) in the Linnean system are kingdom, phylum, class, order, family, genus, and species.

TAXONOMY

Taxonomy is the science of classifying organisms into groups by structure, origin, common ancestor, etc.

TEETH

Teeth are the jagged edges on some leaves, like those of thistles and hawthorne.

TEMPERATE RAINFOREST

Temperate rainforests are very wet, ancient forests that rarely freeze or get very hot. Most of the world's temperate rainforests are in the Pacific Northwest of the USA.

TERMINAL BUD

The terminal bud is a bud located at the apex (tip) of the stem. This type of bud is the dominant bud, since it can cause all the lateral (side) buds below them to remain dormant at all times of the year. Terminal buds have special tissue, called apical meristem, cells that can divide indefinitely.

TERTIARY PERIOD

The Tertiary period lasted from 65 to 1.8 million years ago. It followed the Cretaceous period (the end of the Mesozoic Era) and the K-T extinction. Many mammals developed then, including primitive whales, rodents, pigs, cat, rhinos, etc.

TESTA

The testa is the seed coat. It covers the seed.

TETHYS SEA

The Tethys sea was a shallow sea that existed during the early Mesozoic Era. It was the body of water that separated the landmass of Laurasia in the north from Gondwanaland in the south.

THEORY

A theory is a proposed explanation for a phenomenon.

THIGMOTROPISM

Thigmotropism is the directional bending or turning response of a plant upon contact with a solid surface or object; it is basically a sense of touch in plants. For example, the tendrils of vines are thigmotropic.

THORN

A thorn is a sharp, modified stem. Thorns have a stem-like vascular structure. The honey locust plant has thorns.

THYLAKOID DISK

Thylakoid disks are disk-shaped membrane structures in chloroplasts that contain chlorophyll. Chloroplasts are made up of stacks of thylakoid disks; a stack of thylakoid disks is called a granum. Photosynthesis (the production of ATP molecules from sunlight) takes place on thylakoid disks. Thylakoid means 'sac-like' in Greek.

TIPITI

A tipiti is a flexible braided cylindrical basket made of jacitara palm bark that is used by the Tupis of South America. The tipiti is used to remove the poison liquid from bitter cassava root. The cassava pulp is squeezed in the tipiti until the poisonous liquid is extracted. This process makes the cassava edible.

TOMATO

The tomato is scientifically considered to be a fruit (because the seeds of the plant are contained within the tomato).

TRACE FOSSILS

Also known as ichnofossils, these are fossilized footprints, nests, dung, gastroliths, etc., but not actual body parts. They record the movement and behavior of animals.

TRACHEOPHYTE

A tracheophyte is a plant with true vascular tissue, like xylem and phloem.

TRANSGRESSION

Transgression is the flooding of a continent as the sea level increases, usually caused by melting polar ice. Another cause is sea floor spreading and underwater volcanism, in which large amounts of underwater lava cause water to be displaced onto land.

TRANSPIRATION

Transpiration is the process in which plants lose water through pores in their leaves (these openings are called stomata). As water is lost from the plant, the plant takes up more water (and minerals) through its roots. The rate of transpiration varies as the conditions of the plant change and is controlled by the opening and closing the stomata.

TREE

A tree is a plant that produces wood (made by xylem cells). These tall plants grow taller each year.

TREE FERN

Tree ferns are tall vascular plants that live in warm climates. These ferns have a clump of fronds on top of a fibrous trunk.

TREE RINGS

By counting the number of tree rings in a tree's trunk, you can tell how old the tree was.

TRIASSIC PERIOD

Dinosaurs and mammals evolved during the Triassic period, 248 - 208 million years ago.

TROPHIC LEVEL

A trophic level is a level of the grazing food chain. For example, plant-eaters are primary consumers; they occupy the second trophic level in the grazing food chain.

TROPICAL RAINFOREST

Tropical rainforests are warm, very wet forests that do not freeze (the temperature remains over 75°F=24°C) and do not get extremely hot. Tropical rainforests cover about 7% of the earth's surface, in a band around the equator. They are also called equatorial rainforests.

TROPICS

The tropics are a 3,000 mile (4800 km) wide band around the equator, between the Tropic of Cancer (23.5° N latitude) and the Tropic of Capricorn (23.5° S latitude).

TRUNK

The trunk of a tree is the stem that supports the crown.

TSUNAMI

A tsunami is a huge wave, caused by undersea earthquakes, volcanic eruptions, or, more rarely, by asteroid or meteoroid impact (as in the case of the K-T extinction).

TUBER

A tuber is a modified root that stores nutrients. Potatoes are tubers.

TUMBLEWEEDS

Tumbleweeds are annual plants that have a rounded shape; they dry our in the fall, and the stem beaks off near the ground. The ball-shaped, withered plant tumbles around in the wind (hence the name), scattering their seeds. There are many different types of tumbleweed - they live in the prairie and plains of the United States. One common type of tumbleweed is Russian thistle (*Salsola kali*).

TURGOR PRESSURE

Turgor pressure is the force that is exerted on a plant's cell wall by the water (in the cytoplasm) within the cell. The water presses against the cell wall from within, giving the plant cell rigidity, helping it keep its shape. Turgor pressure is the mechanism that changes the shape of the guard cells that open a plant's stomata, pores located on the underside of leaves.

TUSSOCK GRASS

Tussock grass (*Deschampsia cespitosa* or *Aira cespitosa*) is a tall variety of grass (20 to 36 inches tall) that is used as an ornamental grass. Tussock grass grows in clumps and has fine hair-like leaves. In summer it produces fine green to yellow inflourences.

TYPE SPECIES

A type species is the species of an organism from which a new genus is named. For example, Tyrannosaurus rex is the type species for the genus Tyrannosaurus.

TYPE SPECIMEN

A type specimen is the set of fossil remains of an organism from which a new species is named.

U

UNDERSTORY

The understory of a rainforest is a dark, cool environment under the leaves in the trees (the canopy) of a forest, but over the ground.

UNICELLULAR

Unicellular organisms consist of a single cells.

URANIUM 235

Uranium 235 is a radioactive element; over time, it gradually changes into the element lead. It can be used to date very old rock layers.

V

VACUOLE

A vacuole is a large, membrane-bound space within a plant cell that is filled with fluid. Most plant cells have a single vacuole that takes up much of the cell. It helps maintain the shape of the cell.

VASCULAR PLANT

A vascular plant has specialized pipelines that carry water and nutrients around the plant. Club mosses, ferns, horestails, gymnosperms, and flowering plants are vascular plants.

VASCULAR TISSUE

Vascular tissue is tissue that transports water and nutrients through a plant. Xylem and phloem are types of vascular tissue.

VEGETABLES

A vegetable is a plant whose stem, leaves, tubers, roots, bulbs, or flower is a food source for people. Some examples of vegetables include carrots, eggplant, potatoes, spinach, broccoli, onion, and asparagus.

VEGETATION

Vegetation is all of the plant life found in an area.

VEGETATIVE PROPAGATION

Vegetative propagation is a method of reproducing asexually; the offspring have the same genetic makeup as the parent.

VEGETATIVE STATE

The vegetative state is the stage in a flowering plant's life cycle before the appearance of its fruiting structures.

VEIN

A vein is a vascular structure (xylem and phloem cells surrounded by the bundle sheath) in a leaf that provides supports for the leaf and transports both water and food. The veins on monocots are almost parallel to the margins of the leaf. The veins of dicots radiate from a central midrib.

VEINLET

A veinlet is a small vein. Veinlets are located toward the margins of the leaf.

VENATION

Venation is the arrangement of veins in a leaf. Some different cenation patterns include pinnate, palmate (illustrated above), and parallel

VENDIAN

The Vendian or Ediacaran period was a geologic time period that lasted from 650 to 544 million years ago. The Vendian is when the earliest-known animals evolved. Vendian biota (Ediacara fauna), included soft-bodied multi-cellular animals, like sponges. During the Vendian, the continents had merged into a single supercontinent called Rodinia. The Vendian ended in a mass extinction.

VENUS FLYTRAP

The Venus flytrap is a plant that catches and digests bugs. Classification: Division Magnoliophyta (angioperms), Class Magnoliopsida (dicots), Subclass Dilleniidae, Order Nepenthales (insectivorous plants), Family Droseraceae (Sundews and Venus Flytrap).

VINE

A vine is a plant that needs support as it grows. Some vines grow by twining around other objects for support (e.g., morning glory), some use tendrils (modified shoots)

to attach to objects (e.g., peas and vetch), and others send out aerial roots, often with suckers (e.g., poison ivy).

VOLCANO

When a volcano erupts, it spews out lava and gases from deep inside the earth. Radioisotope dating lava layers in rock sediment enables scientists to establish the date of fossils.

WATER CYCLE

The water cycle (also known as the hydrologic cycle) is the journey water takes as it circulates from the earth's surface to the sky and back again.

WAXY CUTICLE

The cuticle is the fatty or waxy outer layer of epidermal cells that are above ground.

WEALDEN FORMATION

The Wealden Formation is an area in southeastern England (including the Isle of Wight) that had yielded many fossils, iincluding dinosaurs. Paleontologist Gideon Mantell found Iguanodon there in 1825. The Wealden sedimentary rock dates from the Early Cretaceous period, when the area had fresh and brackish water (slightly salty) sediments.

WEGENER, ALFRED L.

Alfred Lothar Wegener (1880-1930), the German geologist and meteorologist, proposed the theory of continental drift in his 1915 book, *On the Origin of Continents and Oceans*. This theory states that parts of the earth's crust slowly drift atop a liquid core. The fossil record overwhelmingly supports and gives credence to the theory of continental drift (and that of plate tectonics). He proposed the existence of the supercontinent Pangaea, and named it (Pangaea means "all the land" in Greek). Wegener froze to death while heading an expedition crossing the Greenland ice cap in 1930.

WELWITSCHIA

Welwitschia mirabilis is an unusual, long-lived, succulent gymnosperm. This plant has a low, two-lobed trunk, and two large, straplike leaves that sprawl along the ground. The plant only produces two leaves, but the wind splits them into many segments. It has a large, deep taproot. Welwitschia produces either male or female cones (but not both). Welwitschia lives in coastal desert areas, gravel beds, rocky canyon walls, and open flats. It derives its moisture from the morning fog. It is found from Namibia to southwestern Angola (in southwestern Africa). It has a life span of over 1,500 years. Welwitschia was first discovered by (and is named for) the Austrian botanist Dr. Friedrich Welwitsch in 1859. Classification: Division Pinophyta (Gymnosperms), Subdivision Gneticae, Class Gnetopsida, Order Gnetales, Family Welwitschiaceae (Welwitschia)m Genus Welwitschia, Species *W. mirabilis*.

WILLIAMSONIA

Williamsonia is a fossil plant that thrived from the Triassic period through the Cretaceous period. Williamsonia was a bennettitalean (a cycadeoidphyte, a primitive gymnosperm that resembled cycads but was not a cycad). Williamsonia had a long, thin, branching, woody trunk covered with spirals of broken-off leaf scars. It was up to 6.5 ft (2 m) tall.

WISCONSIN FAST PLANTS

Wisconsin fast plants are fast-growing plant varieties that were developed at the University of Wisconsin, Madison, Wisconsin, USA. Fast plants complete their life cycles about 45 days after planting. Fast plants are used in classrooms and laboratories around the world for teaching and research. The first plants in space were Fast plants.

WOOD

Wood is the secondary xylem of gymnosperms and dicots, but the term wood is often applied to other xylem. Wood is used to make furniture, build houses, and make paper.

XERIC

Xeric environmental conditions are ones that are very dry.

XEROPHYTE

A xerophyte is a plant that is adapted to very dry conditions (like deserts and the emergent level of the rainforest). Succulents, bromeliads and cacti are xerophytes. Their adaptations include small or absent leaves, small, sunken stomata, and thick cuticles.

XYLEM

Xylem is a tissue in plant stems and roots. Xylem transports water and minerals upwards from the roots to the stem, via capillary action. Xylem is strong and also provides support to the plant.

Y

YUCCA

Yucca is a plant in the agave family that has stiff, sword-like leaves and clusters of white or purplish waxy flowers. This succulent plant is pollinated by the yucca moth. The Joshua tree (*Y. brevifolia*) is a type of yucca. Classification: Division Magnoliophyta, Class Liliopsida (monocots), Subclass Lilidae, Order Liliales, Family Agavaceae (Agaves), Genus Yucca, many species.

Z

ZINNIA

Zinnias are a genus of flowering annual plants that are native to Mexico. Zinnias are named for J.G. Zinn (1727-1759), a German botanist.

ZYGOTE

A zygote is a diploid cell formed by the union of two gametes. It results from the union of an egg cell and a sperm cell.

GLOSSARY OF TECHNICAL TERMS IN PLANT PATHOLOGY

A

Abaxial. Directed away from the stem of a plant; pertaining to the lower surface of a leaf.

Abiotic. Non-living; of non-biological origin.

Abscission. Of plants: The shedding of leaves or other parts as the result of physical weakness in a specialized layer of cells (abscission layer) that develops at the base.

Acerose. Needle-shaped, like pine needles.

Acervulus. A mass of closely clustered conidiophores and conidia not covered by fungal tissue, initially subcuticular or subepidermal but eventually exposed.

Acropetal. Describes the development of structures (such as spores) in succession from the base towards the apex.

Actinomycetes. (literally "ray fungi") filamentous bacteria that have sometimes been classified as Fungi Imperfecti. Actinomycetes typically are saprobes (especially in soil) but a few are pathogenic to man, animals, and plants.

Acute. 1. Developing suddenly, severe (with reference to disease symptoms). 2. Less than 90 degrees (with reference to an angle).

Adanal. (Nematology) Pertaining to a bursa that does not envelop the entire tail.

Adaxial. Directed toward the stem of a plant; pertaining to the upper surface of a leaf.

Adjuvant. Material added to improve some chemical or physical property (e.g., of a plant protectant) or a biological property (e.g., to improve antibody response to an antigen).

Adnate. (Mycology) of gills or tubes broadly attached to the stipe; attached by nearly the entire width of the gills or layer of tubes.

Aecidium. An aecium with a cup-like outer wall.

Aeciospore. A dikaryotic "transfer" spore of the Uredinales, formed in an aecium on the alternate host in macrocyclic rusts and infecting only the primary host; spores of Stage I in heteroecious or autoecious rusts.

Aecium. In the Uredinales the first sorus that is formed after plasmogamy and bears binucleate aeciospores (Stage I heteroecious or autoecious rusts).

Aerobe. An organism that requires free oxygen for respiration.

Aerobic. With the qualities of an aerobe.

Agar. Mixture of polysaccharides derived from red algae that forms a gel at temperatures below about 40C. Used as a support medium, when supplemented by appropriate buffers and/or nutrients and other ingredients, for the production of microbial cultures, overlaying tissue culture cells, electrophoresis, etc.

Agarose. One of the constituents of agar. Often used in preference to agar because it gels at a lower temperature and does not contain the inhibitors of virus growth frequently present in agar. It is also used widely in gel electrophoresis because it has a more uniform pore size than that of agar.

Agent of Disease. An organism or abiotic factor that causes disease; a pathogen.

Agent of Inoculation. That which transports inoculum from its source to or into the infection court (e.g., wind, splashing rain, insects, humans).

Agglutination. The formation of insoluble aggregates following the combination of antibodies with cells or other particulate antigens or with soluble antigens bound to cells or other particles or following the combination of soluble (or particulate) antigens with cell-bound or particle-bound antibodies.

Aggressiveness. Of a plant pathogen: relative ability to colonize and cause damage to plants. See also virulence. (Note: The Federation of British Plant Pathologists, now the British Society for Plant Pathology, has rejected this term and considered it to be synonymous with pathogenicity.)

Alae. (Nematology) Expansions or projections formed by a longitudinal thickening of the cuticle of a nematode. Cervical alae are confined to the anterior region of nematodes parasitic in animals. Caudal alae occur in the posterior region of males in a number of genera. Longitudinal alae, usually four, extend the length of the body sublaterally.

Allantoid. Of spores: sausage-shaped; somewhat curved, with rounded ends.

Allele. (**allelomorph**). Any of one or more alternative forms of a given gene; both (or all) alleles of a given gene are concerned with the same trait or characteristic, but a particular allele codes for a product qualitatively and/or quantitatively different from that coded by other alleles of that gene.

Alternative host. A plant other than the main host that a parasite can colonize; alternative hosts are not required for completion of the developmental cycle of the parasite.

Amerospore. A non-septate spore.

Amerosporous. Having one-celled spores.

Amphid. In nematodes: A chemosensory organ, occurring laterally in pairs, located in the anterior region. Sometimes called lateral organs.

Amphidelphic. In nematodes: Having two ovaries, one directed anteriorly and the other posteriorly.

Amphigynous. In fungi: Having an antheridium through which the oogonial initial grows.

Amphimictic. In nematodes: 1. Reproduction in which sperm and eggs come from separate individuals (cross-fertilization). 2. Capable of interbreeding freely and of producing fertile offspring.

Amphiospore. Urediniospore with thickened walls and capable of hibernating.

Amplification. Production of multiple copies of a DNA sequence, either in vivo or in vitro, starting with one or a few copies.

Ampulliform. Flask-like in form.

Amyloid. Of spore walls, spore ornamentation, hyphal walls, ascus tips, etc.: Staining blue or grayish to blackish-violet in Melzer's reagent, presumably because of the presence of starch or a starch-like compound.

Anaerobic. Not requiring free, molecular oxygen for respiration.

Anamorph. An asexual (usually conidial) stage in the life cycle of a fungus.

Anastomosis. (= **hyphal fusion**). Fusion of somatic hyphae; characteristic of most Dikaryomycota.

Aneuploid. Chromosome constitution differing from the usual diploid constitution by loss or duplication of chromosomes or chromosomal segments.

Angiocarpous. Of basidium-producing organs: Hymenial surface at first exposed but later covered by an incurving pileus margin and/or excresences from the stipe.

Annule. Thickened interval between transverse striae in the cuticle of a nematode.

Annulus. A membraneous skirt surrounding the stipe of a hymenomycete or gasteromycete.

Antagonism. An ecological association between organisms in which one or more of the participants is harmed or has its activities limited.

Antagonist. An agent or substance that counteracts the action of another.

Antagonistic symbiosis. Parasitism; one organism of an association beefits at the expense of the other.

Antheridium. A male gametangium.

Anthocyanescence. Having reddish-purple color in tissues that are normally green; often a symptom of plant disease appearing in the nearly dead margins around completely dead spots in green leaves.

Anthracnose. Any of various plant diseases, particularly those caused by fungi of the Melanconiales, in which discrete, dark-colored, necrotic lesions develop on the leaves, stems, and/or fruits.

Antibiosis. An association between two organisms that is detrimental to the vital activities of one of them.

Antibiotic. Substance used to inhibit the growth of micro-organisms, including bacteria and fungi.

Antibody. Any immunoglobulin molecule produced in direct response to an antigen and which can combine specifically, non-covalently, and reversibly with the antigen which elicited its formation.

Antigen. Molecule of carbohydrate or protein which stimulates the production of an antibody, with which it reacts specifically.

Antiserum. The serum from a vertebrate that has been exposed to an antigen and which contains antibodies that react specifically with the antigen.

Apiculate. Having an apical point or apiculus.

Apiculus. A short, sharp, but not stiff, point, usually as the bud of a spore.

Apothecium. An ascus-bearing structure (ascocarp) in which the ascus-producing layer (hymenium) is not covered by fungal tissue at maturity.

Appressorium. An enlargement on a hypha or germ tube that attaches itself to the host before penetration takes place.

Arbuscule. Of vesicular-arbuscular mycorrhizae: a much-branched, microscopic haustorial structure of the fungal symbiont that forms within living cortical cells of the root. The interface of the arbuscule with the plant protoplast is a site of exchange of nutrients and growth-regulating chemicals.

Arcuate. Curved like a bow.

Areolated. Divided into small spaces or areolations; usually pertains to the cuticle of a nematode.

Areolation. A condition in which the transverse body annulation of a nematode traverses the lateral field.

Arthrospore. A spore resulting from the fragmentation of a hypha, as in the conidial stage of many Basidiomycetes.

Ascigerous. Of fungi: having asci.

Ascocarp. Ascospore-bearing, multicellular sporocarp formed by a member of the Ascomycotina.

Ascoconidium. A budded spore arising from an ascospore within an ascus.

Ascogenous hypha. The restricted dikaryophase of many Ascomycetes; a dikaryotic hypha that grows out from the fertilized ascogonium.

Ascogonium. In Ascomycetes: the female gametangium; it may be unicellular or multicellular, simple or complex in form.

Ascohymenial. Of, pertaining to, or having the characteristics of the Ascohymeniales.

Ascohymeniales. Ascomycetes having asci (and paraphyses) developing as a hymenium and not in a preformed stroma.

Ascolocular. Of, pertaining to, or having the characteristics of the Loculoascomycetes, the loculate Ascomycetes.

Ascoma. Synonymous with ascocarp.

Ascomycete. Fungus of the subdivision Ascomycotina. In some taxonomic schemes these fungi form the class Ascomycetes.

Ascomycotina. A subdivision of fungi characterized by the formation of sexually derived spores (ascospores) in asci.)

Ascophore. A structure bearing asci (e.g., an ascus-producing hypha).

Ascospore. A spore borne in an ascus.

Ascostroma. A fructification of the Ascomycetes consisting of an undifferentiated mass of tissue or stroma on or in which the asci are developed.

Ascus. A cell that is the site of meiosis and in which endogenous spores (usually meiospores but sometimes also ascoconidia) are formed.

Aseptate. Lacking septa (nonseptate).

Asporogenous. Not capable of forming spores.

Autoecious. Capable of completing a life cycle on one host.

Autotrophic. Capable of growth independent of outside sources of nutrients or growth factors.

Auxotroph. A strain of microorganism lacking the ability to synthesize one or more essential growth factors.

Avirulent. Not exhibiting virulence; nonpathogenic.

Avoidance. Principle of plant disease control marked by deliberate actions to take advantage of environmental factors and time unfavorable for disease development.

Axial. Belonging to, around, in the direction of, or along an axis.

Azygospore. A parthenogenetic zygospore; formed by some vesicular-arbuscular mycorrhizal fungi (family Endogonaceae).

B

Bacillar. Shaped like a short rod.

Bacilliform. Rod-shaped.

Bacillus. 1. A member of the genus *Bacillus*. 2. Any rod-shaped bacterial cell, i.e., a cell whose length is ca. two or more times greater than its width.

Backcross. To cross (mate) with one parent.

Bactericidal. Lethal to bacteria.

Bactericide. A substance that kills bacteria.

Bacteriocin. A protein antibiotic, one or more types of which can be produced and "exported" (excreted) by certain strains of bacteria.

Bacteriophage. A virus that replicates inside a bacterium.

Bacteriostatic. Able to inhibit the growth and reproduction of at least some types of bacteria.

Ballistospore. A spore that when mature is actively projected.

Basidiocarp. A sporocarp produced by a member of the Basidiomycotina and which bears basidiospores.

Basidiole. A structure in the hymenium of a member of the Basidiomycotina that is morphologically similar to a basidium without sterigmata. It may be an immature basidium or a permanently sterile structure in the hymenium.

Basidiomycete. A fungus of the Basidiomycotina.

Basidiomycotina. A subdivision of fungi characterized by the formation of basidiospores on basidia.,

Basidiospore. An exogenous sexual spore (meiospore) borne on a basidium.

Basidium. A cell in which karyogamy and meiosis take place and which bears exogenous spores of sexual origin.

Basipetal. Successive from apex to base.

Bifurcate. Dividing into two branches.

Binary Fission. Fission in which two cells, usually of similar size and shape, are formed by the growth and division of one cell.

Bioassay. Any quantitative procedure in which a given organism is used for assay purposes.

Biological Control. The deliberate use by humans of one species of organism to eliminate or control another.

Biotroph. An organism that derives nutrients from the living tissues of another organism (its host).

Biotype. A subspecies of organism morphologically similar to but physiologically different from other members of the species.

Bipolar. At both ends or poles.

Biseptate. Having two septa.

Bitunicate. Having two walls.

Blastic. One of two basic kinds of conidiogenesis; there is a marked enlargement of a recognizable conidium before it is delimited by a septum.

Blasting. A symptom of plant disease characterized by shedding of unopened buds; classically, the failure to produce fruit or seed.

Blastospore. A spore that arises by budding, as in yeasts.

Blight. A disease characterized by rapid and extensive death of plant foliage. A general term applied to any of a wide range of unrelated plant diseases. (e.g., chestnut blight, fireblight, late blight, halo blight).

Blotch. A disease characterized by large, and irregular in shape, spots or blots on leaves, shoots, and stems.

Blotting. Following electrophoresis: the transfer of nucleic acids and/or proteins from a gel strip to a specialized, chemically reactive matrix on which the nucleic acids, etc. may become covalently bound in a pattern similar to that present in the original gel.

Broadcast application. Application by spreading or scattering on the soil surface.

Broom. In plant pathology: A symptom in which lateral branches proliferate in a dense cluster on the main branch (witches'-broom).

Broth. In microbiology: Any of a variety of liquid media, especially nutrient broth or any liquid medium based on nutrient broth and/or hydrolysed protein.

Buccal capsule. In nematodes: Structure connecting the oral opening with the anterior portion of the esophagus. The buccal capsule (also called the stoma) is subject to great variation among different nematodes.

Bullae. In nematodes: Blisterlike prominences near the vulval fenestra of some Heteroderidae.

Bursa. In nematodes: Caudal alae of males used to clasp the female during copulation.

C

Caeoma. An aecium in the Uredinales that is not surrounded by a peridium; from the form genus *Caeoma*.

Callus. A mass of thin-walled, undifferentiated plant cells, developed as the result of wounding or culture on nutrient media.

Canker. An imprecise term usually used for a plant disease characterized (in woody plants) by the death of cambium tissue and resulting loss and/or malformation of bark, or (in non-woody plants) by the formation of sharply delineated, dry, necrotic, localized lesions on the stem. The term "canker" may also be used to refer to the lesion itself, particularly in woody plants.

Capillitium. A mass of sterile fibers interspersed among spores within a sporocarp (in the Gasteromycetes and Myxomycota).

Capitulum. In nematodes: Medial ventral sclerotization of the spicular pouch.

Capsid. The protein shell that surrounds the virus nucleic acid.

Capsule. In bacteria: A layer of material external to but contiguous with the cell wall.

Cardia. In nematodes: Valvular apparatus connecting the esophagus and intestine. Sometimes called the cardiac valve or esophago-intestinal valve.

Carlavirus. Siglum of carnation latent virus. Member of a group of plant viruses with slightly flexuous, rod-shaped particles containing a single molecule of linear RNA, most of which are transmitted by aphids in a noncirculative manner.

Carmovirus. (Siglum of carnation mottle virus.) Member of a group of plant viruses with small, isometric particles containing a single molecule of linear RNA, transmitted in nature through soil and (rarely) by an insect vector.

Carrier. An organism that bears an infectious agent internally but shows no marked symptoms of the disease caused by that agent.

Caudal. In nematodes: Pertaining to or located near the posterior region or tail.

Causal Agent of Disease. That which is capable of causing disease.

Cell Cycle. The period from one cell division to the next.

Cephalic. In nematodes: Pertaining to or located near the head.

Cephalids. In nematodes: Two structures (posterior and anterior) situated in the cephalic region and extending in a complete circle around the body; possibly part of the nervous system. Sometimes called hypodermal commisures.

Cfu. Colony-forming unit.

Chemotherapy. The use of chemical(s) (e.g., antibiotics or fungicides) for the treatment of a disease.

Chlamydospore. A thick-walled, nonsexual spore; a transformed hyphal cell.

Chloranemia. The necrotic symptom of yellowing; a loss of chlorophyll.

Chlorosis. The loss of chlorophyll from the tissues of a plant, resulting from microbial infection, viral infection, the action of certain phytotoxins, the lack of light, to magnesium or iron deficiency, etc. Chlorotic tissues commonly appear yellowish.

Chord. In nematodes: A longitudinal internal thickening of the hypodermis.

Circulative transmission. Virus transmission characterized by a long period of acquisition of the virus by a vector, a latent period of several hours before the vector is able to transmit the virus, and retention of the virus by the vector for a long period, usually several days.

Cirrhus. (Also **cirrus**.) 1. A mass of spores in the form of a ribbon or tendril, forced from the fruiting body of a fungus. 2. A discrete group of somatic cilia (several to over 100) that act primarily as a unified locomotive organelle; the typical cirrus is conical.

Clamp connection. A recurving outgrowth of a cell that, at cell division, acts as a bridge to allow passage of one of the products of nuclear division into the penultimate cell, thereby assuring maintenance of the dikaryotic condition (of members of the Basidiomycotina).

Clavate. Club-shaped.

Cleistothecium. An ascocarp with the asci surrounded by fungal tissue and without regularly formed openings.

Cloaca. In nematodes: A common duct or cavity in which the digestive and reproductive systems terminate in males.

Clone. 1. (n.) (a) A population of recombinant DNA molecules all carrying the same inserted sequence; (b) a colony of micro-organisms containing a specific DNA fragment inserted into a vector; (c) a population of cells or organisms of identical genotype. 2. (v.) (a) the use of in vitro recombination techniques to insert a particular DNA sequence into a vector; (b) the selection of a unique virus isolate from individual plaques, pocks or lesions or by limiting dilution; (c) the vegetative propagation of an organism to produce a population of identical individuals.

Cloning. An in vitro procedure in which a particular sequence of DNA (e.g., a gene) is reproduced in large amounts by inserting ("splicing") it into a suitable replicon, introducing the resultant recombinant (hybrid) molecule into a cell in which it can replicate, and finally growing the cells in culture.

Closterovirus. (From Greek *kloster*, "thread") Member of a group of plant viruses with very long, flexuous, rod-shaped particles containing a single molecule of linear RNA, some members of which are transmitted by whiteflies.

Cluster Cup. Aecidium.

Coalesce. To merge or grow together into a similar but larger structure.

Coccus A spherical (or near-spherical) bacterial cell.

Codon. A particular sequence of three nucleotides in mRNA coding for an amino acid.

Coelomycetes. A group of the Deuteromycetes producing pycnidia or acervuli.

Coenocyte. A multinucleate cell; a protoplast in which the nuclear divisions have not been followed by cytoplasmic cleavage.

Coenocytic. Multinucleate or without cross walls.

Coenozygote. A cell containing more than one zygote.

Commensalism. Symbiosis in which neither organism is injured; one or neither may be benefited.

Commisure. In nematodes: Connecting bands of nerve tissue.

Comovirus. (Siglum of cowpea mosaic virus). Member of a group of multicomponent plant viruses with small, isometric particles containing two linear RNA species, readily transmitted mechanically and by beetles.

Compartmentalization. In trees: the processes that result in isolation of wounded or diseased xylem from normal xylem by the formation of chemically and anatomically specialized tissue around the damaged zone.

Competition. A more or less active demand on the part of two organisms for some commodity (space, food, etc.) that is inadequate to provide for all organisms present.

Conidiogenesis. Conidium formation.

Conidiogenous cell. A conidium-producing cell.

Conidioma A specialized, multi-hyphal structure bearing conidia.

Conidiophore. A hypha, often specialized in structure, that bears one or more conidia.

Conidium. A thin-walled, asexual spore that is borne exogenously on a conidiophore and is deciduous at maturity.

Conjugate. To carry out conjugation.

Conjugation. In general, any of various sexual processes in microorganisms in which gene transfer follows the establishment of direct contact between two (or more) cells which typically show little or no morphological differentiation from vegetative cells. In bacterial conjugation, one bacterium (the "male" or donor cell) transfers DNA to another (the "female" or recipient cell) while the cells are in physical contact; a recipient that has received DNA from a donor is called a transconjugant.

Conk. The basidiocarp of a wood-decaying fungus, usually a polypore.

Context. The inner or body tissue of a fruit body which supports the hymenophore in the larger and especially the pileate species of Hymenomycetes.

Control. Economic reduction of crop losses caused by plant diseases.

Cornute. Horned; horn-like.

Corpus. In nematodes: The anterior cylindrical part of the esophagus. The basal region of the corpus at times may be swollen to form a bulb.

Coryneform. 1. Essentially rod-shaped with one end thickened or bulbous. 2. A name applied, loosely, to any Gram-positive, asporogenous, pleomorphic rod-shaped bacterium; as such it covers bacteria from a range of genera.

Cosmid. A plasmid into which has been inserted the *cos* site of bacteriophage.

Crop rotation. The practice of growing a sequence of different crops on the same land in successive years or seasons; done to replenish the soil, curb pests, etc.

Cross-protection. The protection conferred on a host by infection with one strain of a virus that prevents infection by a closely-related strain.

Crozier formation. Process of ascus development from coiled tips of ascigerous hyphae.

Crozier. A recurved hook at the tip of an ascogenous hypha, the penultimate cell of which will become the ascus.

Crustaformeria. In nematodes: Glandular region of the distal part of uterus that may play a role in the formation of the egg envelope; sometimes called the quadricolumella.

Cucumovirus. Siglum of cucumber mosaic virus. Member of a group of multicomponent plant viruses with isometric (icosahedral) particles consisting of three linear RNA species (RNAs 1, 2, and 3), transmitted by sap and in nature by aphids in a noncirculative manner.

Cultivar. A cultivated plant variety or cultural selection.

Culture collection. A repository of cultures of characterized viruses, bacteria, and other organisms. Used for reference and comparison with new isolates.

Culture. 1. To grow an organism. 2. the resulting growth. Usually on artificial medium.

Cupulate. Cup-shaped.

Cuticle. 1. A thin, waxy layer on the outer wall of epidermal cells consisting primarily of wax and cutin. 2. Noncellular exterior covering of nematodes.

Cutin. An insoluble polymer that, embedded in waxes, forms the cuticle covering the epidermal cell walls in the aerial parts of higher plants.

Cutinolytic. Of certain enzymes: able to digest cutin.

Cutis. Of basidiocarps of certain wood-decaying fungi: the outer layer consisting of compressed hyphae parallel to the surface, sometimes with varnishlike incrustation.

Cylindrical. Of the stipe, spores, etc.: Of the same diameter throughout the length.

Cyst. In fungi: An encysted zoospore. In nematodes: the egg-containing carcass of dead adult females of the genus Heterodera or Globodera.

Cystidium A sterile cell occurring among basidia and often projecting beyond the hymenium, differing morphologically from the basidium.

Cytokinins. Phytohormones that stimulate metabolism and cell division.

D

Damping-off. A disease that results in the collapse and death of seedlings before or after they emerge from the soil (pre-emergence and post-emergence damping-off, respectively). Common causal agents include species of *Pythium* and *Rhizoctonia*.

Decay. The gradual decomposition of dead organic matter.

DEGO. Dorsal Esophageal Gland Outlet. In nematodes: The point at which the dorsal gland empties into the lumen of the esophagus.

Deirid. In nematodes: Paired, porelike organs located in the lateral fields, in the vicinity of the nerve ring of many of the Tylenchoidea; believed by some workers to be sensory in nature.

Denticle. In nematodes: Minute tooth or "prickle".

Dermatophyte. A parasitic fungus that attacks and causes a disease of the skin.

Desiccate. To dry out.

Determinate. Having a fixed, definite limit.

Deuteromycete. A member of the Deuteromycotina.

Deuteromycotina. A non-phylogenetic category originally created for fungi with no known sexual stage; the category still includes fungi with no known sexual stage, but it also includes the asexual stages of various fungi now known to have a sexual stage in the Ascomycotina or Basidiomycotina.

Dextrinoid. (Of spores, etc.) stained yellowish- or reddish-brown by Melzer's iodine.

Diagnostic. A distinguishing characteristic important in the identification of a disease or other disorder.

Dichotomous. Dividing into two equal branches.

Dictyospore. A spore divided by intersecting septa in more than one plane.

Dictyosporous. Having spores with cross and longitudinal walls.

Didelphic. Of nematodes: Possessing two complete genital tubes or ovaries.

Didymospore. A spore with one transverse septum.

Didymosporous. Having two-celled spores.

Dieback. Progressive death of shoots, branches and roots generally starting at the tip.

Differential host. A plant host that on the basis of disease symptoms serves to distinguish between various strains or races of a given plant pathogen.

Dikaryon. A pair of nuclei that associate and divide simultaneously.

Dikaryotic. The condition of containing a dikaryon.

Dimorphic. Producing two morphologically different forms.

Dimorphism. Existence of two morphologically different forms in one organism.

Dioecious. Having male and female reproductive structures on separate thalli.

Diorchic. In nematodes: Possessing two testes.

Diploid. Having a ploidy of two.

Disc. Of Valsa and related fungi: a more or less flat apical part of a stroma that protrudes above the bark surface; also, of Discomycetes: the exposed fertile portion of an apothecium.

Discomycetes. A group of the Ascomycetes in which the hymenium is exposed at maturity; one in which the fruiting body is an apothecium or discocarp.

Disease. An abnormal condition of a plant in which its physiology, morphology, and/or development is altered under the continuous influence of a pathogen.

Disease cycle. Of a disease caused by a biotic agent: the cyclical sequence of host and parasite development and interaction that result in disease, in reproduction or replication of the pathogen, and in the readying of a new generation of the parasite for infection.

Disinfectant. A physical or chemical agent that frees a plant, organ, or tissue from infection.

Disinfest. To kill pathogens that have not yet initiated disease, but that occur in or on such inanimate objects as soil, tools, etc., or that occur on the surface of such plant parts as seed.

Disinfestant. An agent that kills or inactivates pathogens in the environment or on the surface of a plant or plant organ before infection takes place.

Dispersal. Spread of a pathogen within an area of its graphical range.

Dissemination. See dispersal.

DNA fingerprinting. A laboratory technique in which the banding patterns of DNA fragments from two different individuals are compared.

DNA polymerase. An enzyme that synthesizes a daughter strand(s) of DNA (under direction from a DNA template). May be involved in repair or replication.

DNA replicase. A DNA-synthesizing enzyme required specifically for replication.

DNA. Deoxyribonucleic acid.

DNAase. An enzyme that attacks bonds in DNA.

Dorsal. Back or upper surface.

Downy mildew. Plant disease caused by certain members of the Peronosporales. Downy mildews are characterized by the formation of superficial hyphal growth in which, typically, individual spore-bearing structures can be distinguished.

E

Echinate. Having sharply pointed spines.

Echinulate. Covered with small spines.

Ectoparasite. A parasite that remains external to the host's cells or tissues.

Ectosymbiosis. Symbiosis in which one member (microsymbiote) develops on the outside of the other member.

Ectotrophic. Refers to a mycorrhiza in which the mycelium forms an external covering on the root.

Eelworm. Nematode.

Effective dissemination. Synonymous with inoculation.

Effuse. Spreading out loosely or flat.

Electrophoresis. A procedure by means of which the members of a heterogenous population of charged particles can be separated by virtue of their dissimilar migration characteristics in an electric field.

Electroporation. A method by which nucleic acids or virus particles can be introduced into protoplasts or cells by creating transient pores in the plasma membrane using an electric pulse.

Elicitor. A molecule produced by the host (or pathogen) that induces a response by the pathogen (or host).

ELISA. Enzyme-linked immunosorbent assay. A highly sensitive immunoassay for specific antibodies or antigens.

Ellipsoid. Having every plane section an ellipse or a circle.

Emarginate. Of gills, notched near the stipe.

Enation. A symptom caused by certain plant viruses in which there are small outgrowths on the plant.

Encysted. Surrounded by a hard shell (cyst).

Endemic. Of a disease: Native to a particular place.

Endoconidiophore. A conidiophore that produces conidia within itself.

Endoconidium. A conidium produced endogenously in a hypha or conidiophore.

Endogenous. Arising from within the generating structure.

Endonuclease. A nuclease which cleaves phosphodiester bonds *within* a nucleic acid strand.

Endoparasite. A parasite that lives intracellularly or within the tissues of the host.

Endosymbiosis. Symbiosis in which one member (microsymbiote) lives within the other.

Endotrophic. Refers to a mycorrhiza in which the mycelium grows within the cortical cells of the root (e.g., in orchids).

Enzyme. A protein produced by living cells that can catalyze a specific organic reaction.

Epidemic. A change in the amount of disease in a population in time and space.

Epidemiology. 1. The study of the interrelationships between a given pathogen, the environment, and groups or populations of the relevant hosts. 2. The study of epidemics.

Epidermis. The superficial layer of cells occurring on all plant parts.

Epinasty. Downward curling of a leaf blade resulting from more rapid cell growth on the upper side of a petiole than on the lower side; often a hyperplastic symptom of plant disease.

Epiparasite. An organism parasitic on another that parasitizes a third.

Epiphyte. An epiphytic organism.

Epiphytic. Growing externally on a plant without parasitizing it.

Epiptygma. In nematodes: A vulval flap.

Epitype. A specimen selected as a standard for a species or lower taxon when all original material except for illustrations has been destroyed.

Eradicant. Any chemical agent that eliminates particular pathogen(s) from diseased plants treated with that agent.

Eradication. Control of plant disease by eliminating the pathogen after it is established or by eliminating the plants that carry the pathogen.

Ergot. Disease of certain grasses and cereals, especially rye, caused by *Claviceps purpurea*; also the spur-shaped sclerotium of *C. purpurea* that replaces the grain in a diseased inflorescence.

Erumpent. Breaking through the surface; bursting forth.

Escape. Failure of inherently susceptible plants to become diseased, even though disease is prevalent.

Esophagus. In nematodes: The portion of the alimentary canal between the buccal capsule, or stoma, and the anterior portion of the intestine.

Ethidium bromide. (2,7-diamino-10-ethyl-9-phenylphenanthridinium bromide). A trypanocidal, bacteriostatic dye that binds to DNA and fluoresces under near-ultraviolet light; used for tracking nucleic acids.

Etiolation. A phenomenon exhibited by plants grown in the dark: etiolated plants are pale yellow and have long internodes and small leaves.

Etiology. The study of cause; that phase of plant pathology dealing with the causal agent and its relations with the susceptible plant.

Exclusion. The principle of plant disease prevention in which the pathogen is prevented from entering a given region.

Excretory pore. In nematodes: The exterior opening of the excretory system, generally located on the ventral side of the body near the basal region of the esophagus; also known as the orifice of the cervical gland.

Excretory. In nematodes: A tube or canal, lined with cuticle, that leads to the excretory pore.

Exogenous. Arising on the outside of the generating structure.

Exonuclease. A nuclease that sequentially removes nucleotides from one end of a strand of nucleic acid.

Exopathogen. Nonparasitic organism whose extracellular toxic metabolites cause disease in plants.

Extracellular. Outside the cells.

Exudate. Material that has passed from within a plant structure to the outer surface or into the surrounding medium; as in leaf exudate, root exudate, etc.

F

Facultative anaerobe. Refers to an organism that normally grows aerobically but can grow anaerobically.

Facultative parasite. An organism that normally lives as a saprophyte but under certain conditions can live as a parasite.

Facultative saprophyte. A mainly parasitic organism with the ability to survive for a part of its life cycle as a saprophyte and be cultured on artificial media.

Falcate. (Of spores) sickle-shaped.

Fallow. Previously cultivated land kept free from crops or weeds during at least one growing season.

Fasciation. Hyperplastic symptoms characterized by a fusing (and flattening) of such plant organs as stems.

Fasciculation. Hyperplastic symptom characterized by a clustering of such plant organs as shoots into such structures as witches' brooms.

Fenestra. In nematodes: A window or transparent spot; in some Heteroderidae, a thin-walled region of the vulval cone.

Fenestrate. Having a fenestra.

Fenestration. The area in which the fenestra occurs.

Fermentation. Oxidation of certain organic substances in the absence of molecular oxygen.

Filiform. Thread-shaped.

Fission. Cell division by cleavage (splitting) of the cell into two parts.

Fitness. The ability of an organism to survive and reproduce; the ability of an organism to pass its genes to the next generation.

Flagellate. Having one or more flagella.

Flagellum. A whip-like appendage responsible for motility in the majority of motile bacteria and other protists, fungi, algae, etc.

Flexure. A turn or fold.

Form genus. A non-phylogenetic category, equivalent to genus, distinguished on the basis of one or more morphological features. In the Deuteromycotina, form genera are used to classify anamorphs; such form genera are based primarily on the characteristics (including mode of development) of the conidia, conidiophores, and conidiomata.

Form species. A non-phylogenetic category, equivalent to species, distinguished on the basis of one or more morphological features of an anamorph, treated as if it were an independent entity, especially for indexing or identification purposes; of importance chiefly in the Ascomycetes and Uredinales.

Forma-specialis. Literally "special form". An infraspecific taxonomic rank in which the taxa are distinguished on a physiological basis, particularly on the basis of adaptation to (or pathogenicity for) one or more specific hosts. In mycology, *forma specialis* is a taxonomic rank lower than form, subvariety, variety and subspecies, and higher than physiological race.

Fructification. 1. Synonymous with fruiting body. 2. The formation or development of a fruiting body.

Fruiting body. Any multi-hyphal structure that bears or contains spores.

Fumigant. A gas or volatile substance that is used to disinfest certain areas of various pests.

Fungicidal. Kills fungi.

Fungicide. A chemical or physical agent that kills or inhibits the growth of fungi. (Note some substances termed "fungicides" are fungistatic in their action.

Fungistasis. Inhibition of fungal growth or reproduction that is not lethal.

Fungistat. A substance that prevents fungal growth without killing the fungus.

Fungistatic. Able to inhibit the growth and/or reproduction of at least some types of fungi.

Fungus. A eukaryotic, heterotrophic organism whose usually walled, threadlike cells absorb nutrients.

Furcate. Forked.

Fusiform. Spindle-shaped; tapering at each end.

G

Gall. An abnormal plant structure formed in response to parasitic attack by certain microorganisms (bacteria, fungi, viruses) or insects. Galls may develop either by localized cell proliferation or increase in cell size.

Gametangium. A structure that contains gametes.

Gamete. A haploid cell or nucleus involved in sexual reproduction, during which two gametes fuse to form a zygote.

Gametogenesis. The development of gametes.

Gasteromycete. A member of the Gasteromycetes.

Gasteromycetes. The group of Basidiomycetes with spores borne in cavities within the fruit body.

Gel. A matrix of polyacrylamide, agarose or similar material in which the electrophoresis of molecules is carried out.

Gel electrophoresis. A type of electrophoresis in which the molecules in a sample moves through a gel composed of agarose or polyacrylamide.

Geminivirus. (From Latin *gemini*, "twins", for the typical double particles). Member of the only group of plant viruses with double particles, each particle containing circular or linear single-stranded DNA; this group is divided into two subgroups I and II (transmitted in a circulative manner by leafhoppers) and subgroup III (transmitted in a circulative manner by whiteflies or, in the case of some viruses in this group, mechanically transmitted).

Gene expression. The transcription of mRNA from the DNA sequence of a gene and the subsequent translation of that mRNA to give the protein gene product. Less strictly it can mean the transcription step alone.

Genetic code. The nucleotide sequence of a DNA molecule (or, in certain viruses, of an RNA molecule) in which information for the synthesis of proteins is contained.

Genital papillae. In nematodes: Tactile or sensory organs located on the male tail.

Genital primordium. In nematodes: The initial cells of the reproductive system.

Genome. The genetic information for an organism, consisting (in the case of viruses) of one or more species of either RNA or DNA, but not both.

Genotype. The genetic constitution of an organism.

Genus. A taxonomic rank above species and below family; the generic name of an organism is the first of the binomial.

Germ tube. A short, hypa-like structure that develops from certain types of spores upon germination.

Germination by repetition. On the germination of a spore, the formation of a secondary spore rather than a germ tube.

Germination. In bacteria or fungi, the process by which a spore gives rise to a vegetative cell or hypha.

Gill. A hymenium-covered, plate-like appendage that hangs from the under surface of the basidiocarp of some Hymenomycetes.

Glaucous. Having a bluish gray waxy surface.

Globose. Spherical, or nearly so.

Gram reaction. The result of the Gram stain.

Gram stain. An important bacteriological staining procedure discovered empirically in 1884 by the Danish scientist Christian Gram. When bacteria are stained with certain basic dyes, the cells of some species (Gram-negative species) can be easily decolorized with organic solvents such as ethanol or acetone. Cells of Gram-positive species resist decolorization.

Gubernaculum. In nematodes: Spicule guide; sclerotized accessory piece.

Guiding ring. In nematodes: Sleeve-like structure that surrounds and guides the stylet in genera of the Dorylaimoidea. Position varies among the genera from near apex to posterior portion of stylet.

Gummosis. A plant disease in which the lesions exude a sticky liquid.

Guttation. Exudation of water from plants, particularly along the leaf margin.

H

Habitat. A place with a particular kind of environment suitable for the growth of an organism.

Haploid. Having a ploidy of one.

Haustorium. A specialized branch of a hypha formed inside a host cell by certain plant-parasitic fungi (especially obligate parasites) in order to obtain nutrients.

Head. In nematodes: That portion anterior to the base of the stoma or stylet.

Helicospore. A cylindric, spiral or convolute spore, usually septate.

Helicosporous. Having spiral or at least strongly curved, often septate, spores.

Hemizonid. In nematodes: Lens-like structure situated between the cuticle and hypodermal layer on the ventral side of the body just anterior to the excretory pore; generally believed to be associated with the nervous system.

Hemizonion. In nematodes: A companion structure to the hemizonid; it is smaller and located posterior to the hemizonid.

Heteroecious. Requiring more than one host species to complete a life cycle (e.g., of Uredinales)

Heterogamy. Plasmogamy between morphologically different gametes.

Heterokaryon. A cell that contains genetically different nuclei or a thallus made up of such cells.

Heterokaryosis. The result of forming a heterokaryon of a fungus; the condition of a hypha or cell having two or more genetically distinct haploid nuclei.

Heterokaryotic. The condition of being a heterokaryon.

Heteroploid. Having a complement of chromosomes differing from that characteristic of the species.

Heterothallic. The condition of being self-sterile, requiring a partner for sexual reproduction.

Heterothallism. The phenomenon in which sexual reproduction requires the involvement of two different thalli.

Heterotopy. Hyperplastic symptom in which an organ develops in a position other than its normal one.

Heterotroph. An organism that obtains its food from other organisms, living or dead.

Heterotrophic. Requiring organic substrates for growth and development; being incapable of synthesizing required organic materials from inorganic sources.

Histopathology. The study of pathology of cells and tissues; the microscopic changes characteristic of disease.

Holobasidium. A single-celled basidium.

Holoblastic. When both outer and inner walls of the conidiogenous cell contribute to the formation of the blastoconidium.

Holocarpic reproduction. In fungi, reproduction in which the entire fungal body is segmented into spores.

Holomorph. Any fungus considered in its entirety, i.e., including all latent or expressed (anamorphic or teleomorphic) forms.

Holotype. The single specimen designated or indicated as "the type" by the original author at the time of publication of the original description.

Homokaryon. A hyphal cell, mycelium, organism, or spore in which all the nuclei are genetically identical.

Homokaryotic. Refers to a homokaryon.

Homothallic. The condition of being self-fertile, able to reproduce sexually without a partner.

Horizontal resistance. In a given cultivar: the existence of similar levels of resistance to each of the races of a given pathogen.

Host. A plant that supports the growth and development of the parasite that has infected it.

Hyaline. Transparent, translucent, or colorless.

Hybrid. The offspring of two individuals differing in one or more heritable characteristics.

Hybridization. 1. In molecular biology: The formation of stable duplexes between complementary sequences by way of Watson-Crick base-pairing. 2. Cross-breeding.

Hydathode. A specialized leaf structure with one or more openings through which water is discharged from the interior of the leaf to its surface.

Hydrosis. Necrotic symptom of disease characterized by water-soaking of tissues.

Hymenium. A palisade-like layer of asci or basidia, including any sterile cells, such as basidioles, paraphyses, or cystidia.

Hymenomycete. A member of the Hymenomycetes.

Hymenomycetes. The group of Basidiomycetes possessing an exposed hymenium.

Hymenophore. Spore-bearing structure; the part of a basidioma bearing the hymenium.

Hyperparasite. A parasite of a parasite.

Hyperplasia. The enlargement of an organ or tissue owing to an increase in the number of cells.

Hypersensitive. The state of being abnormally sensitive. It often refers to an extreme reaction to a pathogen (e.g., the formation of local lesions by a virus or the necrotic response of a leaf to bacterial infection).

Hypersensitivity. The expression of extreme reactivity by a plant in response to a potential parasite or pathogen, the plant's response commonly serving to limit or prevent parasitization/disease.

Hypertrophy. Increase in cell size causing an increase in the size of an organ or tissue.

Hypha. Filamentous part of a fungus, usually septate and consisting of several cells in linear succession.

Hyphal fusion. See anastomosis.

Hyphal peg. 1. A compound, hyphal, fasciculate projection extending beyond the general level of the hymenium, consisting of two or more parallel or interwoven hyphae, encrusted or gelatinized. 2. A projection from a hypha.

Hyphomycetes. A group of the Deuteromycetes without differentiated pycnidia or acervuli.

Hyphopodium. A short branch of one or two cells of the epiphytic mycelium of a black mildew fungus.

Hypodermal. Pertaining to the hypodermis.

Hypodermis. In nematodes: A thin tissue layer beneath the cuticle that thickens to form the dorsal, lateral, and ventral chords, which extend the length of the body.

Hypogeous. Growing below ground.

Hyponasty. More rapid growth of the lower side of an organ than of the upper side.

Hypoplasia. Underdevelopment resulting from an abnormal paucity of cells.

Hypovirulence. A reduced level of virulence in a strain of pathogen resulting from genetic changes in the pathogen or to the effects of an infectious agent on the pathogen.

Hysterothecium. An ascocarp that opens by a slit.

I

Idiomorphs. Nucleotide sequences that occupy the same locus in different strains but are not related in sequence or common descent.

Imbricate. Overlapping, like the shingles of a roof.

Immune. Cannot be infected by a given pathogen.

Immunity. 1. The state of being immune. 2. In plants, the ability to remain free from disease because of inherent structural or functional properties.

Imperfect fungus. See Deuteromycotina.

Imperfect state. The state of a fungus characterized by asexual spores (conidia) or the absence of spores.

In vitro. (Literally "in glass".) Cultivated in an artificial, non-living environment.

In vivo. Within a living organism.

Incipient. Early in development (of a disease or condition).

Incisure. In nematodes: A longitudinal cuticular cleft that divides the lateral fields; sometimes called involution or line.

Incompatible. Not cross-fertile.

Incubation period. The period of time between penetration of a host by a pathogen and the first appearance of symptoms on the host. (2, 24)

Indeterminate. Without definite margin or edge; terminal growth (of hyphae or conidiophores) unrestricted.

Indexing. A procedure to determine whether a given plant is infected by a virus. It involves the transfer of a bud, scion, sap etc. from one plant to one or more kinds of indicator plants sensitive to the virus.

Indicator host. A plant species that gives characteristic symptoms to a specific virus. Used in virus diagnosis.

Infect. Of a parasite: To begin or continue an interactive, usually pathogenic, relationship with the host.

Infection. The interaction of parasite with host; the beginning of that interaction.

Infection court. A site in or on a host plant where infection can occur.

Infection thread. The specialized hypha of a pathogenic fungus that invades tissue of the susceptible plant.

Infectious. Capable of producing propagules that disperse from one host to another and infect it.

Infective. Of an agent of inoculation, capable of transmitting inoculum.

Infest. Of microorganisms and viruses: To contaminate the surface of a plant without establishing an interactive relationship with it; to be present in high numbers in a plant's environment (soil, water, etc.).

Ingress. The act, by a plant pathogen, of gaining entrance into the tissues of a susceptible plant.

Inoculate. To introduce a microorganism into an environment suitable for its growth; to bring a parasite into contact with a host.

Inoculation. The act of inoculating; the placement of microorganisms or viruses at a site where infection is possible (the infection court).

Inoculum. The population of microorganisms introduced in an inoculation; the units of a parasite capable of initiating an infection.

Inoperculate. Of an ascus or a sporangium, opening by a pore or split to discharge spores, as in asci of the Helotiales.

Intercalary. Formed or situated somewhere between apex and base of a given structure.

Intercellular. Between cells.

Intersex. An individual more or less intermediate in phenotype between male and female, displaying secondary male or female characters.

Intracellular. Within or through the cells.

Intumescence. Hyperplastic symptom characterized by blister-like swelling on the surfaces of plant organs.

Invagination. Retraction, under force of pressure, of an outer surface toward the inside.

Invasion. In plant pathology: Spread of a pathogen through tissues of a diseased plant.

Involute. Of the margin of the pileus: Rolled in, especially when young.

Involution. See incisure.

Isoenzyme. See isozyme.

Isogamy. The condition in which gametes are morphologically similar, as in the members of the Zygomycotina. 920)

Isogenic. Two or more organisms or cells having identical genotypes.

Isolate. In plant pathology: a culture or subpopulation of a microorganism separated from its parent population and maintained in some sort of controlled circumstance; also, to effect such separation and control, for example to isolate a pathogen from diseased plant tissue.

Isolation. 1. The process of getting an organism in pure culture. 2. The pure culture itself.

Isoline. (Isogenic line.) One line in a series of genetically similar plant lines that carry different specific genes for resistance to a particular pathogen.

Isotype. Any duplicate of the holotype of a taxon.

Isozyme One of a number of enzymes that catalyse the same reaction(s) but differ from each other in primary structure and/or electrophoretic mobility. (Also isoenzyme.)

Isthmus. In nematodes: Relatively narrow portion of esophagus just anterior to the basal region.

J

Juvenile. The life stage of a nematode between the embryo and the adult; an immature nematode.

Juvenillody. Condition in which tissues and organs remain immature.

K

Karyogamy. The fusion of nuclei.

Karyotype. The chromosomal constitution of a eukaryotic cell in terms of the number, size amd morphology of the chromosomes at metaphase.

Klendusity. A special kind of disease escape in which a susceptible plant avoids disease because of an intrinsic property of the plant itself that greatly reduces the chances of its being inoculated, even though there may be an abundance of inoculum in the area.

Knot. A localized abnormal swelling; a gall.

L

Labial. In nematodes: Pertaining to the lips.

Lamella. See gill.

Latent infection. 1. Infection unaccompanied by visible symptoms. 2. See **latent period**.

Latent period. 1. The period between infection and the appearance of new inoculum. (See incubation period.) 2. Elapsed time between phage infection or induction and lysis of bacterial cells. 3. Period after acquisition of virus by a vector before it becomes infective. (8, 24)

Latent virus. A virus that infects a plant without causing macroscopic symptoms.

Lateral field. In nematodes: An interruption of the transverse striae by longitudinal cuticular thickenings situated on top of the lateral chords. The field is divided by longitudinal striae (incisures) and at times by transverse markings (areolation).

Lateral organs. See amphid.

Leaf spot. A self-limiting lesion on a leaf.

Lectin. A plant protein that binds to certain sugar residues in glycoproteins.

Lectotype. One of a series of syntypes that, after publication of the original description, is selected and designated through publication to serve as the type.

Legitimate. Of taxonomic names and epithets: Published in accordance with the Code of Nomenclature.

Leptoderan. In nematodes: Caudal alae that do not meet posterior to the tail tip.

Lesion. A localized area of diseased or damaged tissue.

Library. In molecular biology: A set of cloned fragments together representing the entire genome.

Lichen. A thallus consisting of an alga and fungus intermixed and living in a symbiotic relationship.

Life cycle. The complete succession of changes undergone by an organism during its life. A new cycle occurs when an identical succession of changes is initiated.

Line. See incisure.

Lips. In nematodes: Cuticular structures (usually six: two subdorsal, two lateral, two subventral) surrounding the mouth opening; lips may be fused in pairs.

Local infection. An infection affecting a limited part of a plant.

Local lesion. A localized spot produced on a leaf upon mechanical inoculation with a virus.

Locular. Containing chambers or hollows.

Locule. A cavity.

Loculoascomycete. A member of the Loculoascomycetes.

Loculoascomycetes. A group of Ascomycotina with bitunicately discharging asci, producing ascospores that are generally septate and borne in unwalled locules (pseudothecia) in ascostromatic ascomata with an ascolocular ontogeny. Not accepted by some authors.

Locus. Site on a chromosome occupied by a particular gene.

Lumen. In nematodes: Triradiate canal or duct of the esophagus. In fungi: The space bounded by tissue or wall, as the central cavity of a cell.

Lunate. Crescent-shaped; half-moon shaped.

Luteovirus. (Literally "yellowish".) Member of a group of plant viruses with isometric particles containing one molecule of linear RNA, mainly confined to the phloem, and usually not mechanically transmitted but transmitted in nature by aphids in a circulative manner.

Lyophilization. Rapid freezing of a material at low temperature followed by rapid dehydration by sublimation in a high vacuum. A method used to preserve biological specimens or to concentrate macromolecules with little or no loss of activity. (Also freeze-drying.)

M

Macroconidium. The larger of two types of conidia formed by certain fungi. *See* microconidium.

Macrocyclic. Of rusts: The two primary spore stages are present (telial with teliospores and aecial with aeciospores).

Macroscopic. Visible to the unaided eye.

Mammillate. Digitate, with nipple-shaped protuberances.

Masked symptoms. Virus-induced plant symptoms that are absent under some environmental conditions but appear when the host is exposed to certain conditions of light and temperature.

Mechanical inoculation. Of plant viruses, a method of experimentally transmitting the pathogen from plant to plant; juice from diseased plants is rubbed on test-plant leaves that usually have been dusted with carborundum or some other abrasive material.

Median bulb. See metacorpus.

Medium. In microbiology: any liquid or solid preparation made specifically for the growth, storage, or transport of microorganisms or other types of cell.

Medulla. Central part of an organ.

Meiosis. The process in which a eukaryotic nucleus divides into nuclei whose ploidy is lower than that of the parent nucleus (typically, haploid nuclei being formed from diploid nuclei) and in which recombination usually occurs.

Meiospore. A uninucleate, haploid spore arising directly by meiosis.

Messenger RNA. A chain of specific ribonucleotides that codes for a specific protein; template for the assembly of amino acids into protein; in cells mRNA is transcribed from DNA, but some RNA viruses function directly as mRNA.

Metabasidium. The cell in which meiosis occurs in members of the Basidiomycotina.

Metacorpus. The swollen posterior portion of the corpus; sometimes called the median bulb.

Metaplasia. Changed condition of a structure or organ; hyperplastic class of symptoms characterized by overdevelopment other than that due to hypertrophy or hyperplasia. (e.g., abnormal starch accumulation, virescence, etc.).

Microconidium. 1. A spermatium. 2. A small conidium. *See* macroconidium.

Microcyclic. A life cycle in the rusts where one or more of the main spore stages, usually the aecial, is absent.

Micropyle. In nematodes: A minute opening in the membrane of an egg through which the spermatozoa enter.

Microsclerotium. A small clump of dark-colored, more or less thick-walled cells, each of which is viable; produced in culture and rarely in the xylem of host plants. (See sclerotium.)

Microscopic. Very small; seen only with the aid of a microscope.

Mildew. A fungal disease of plants in which the mycelium and spores of the fungus are seen as a whitish growth on the host surface.

Minimal medium. A type of culture medium lacking specific growth factors; it does not support the growth of some or all auxotrophic strains of a given organism but permits the growth of prototrophic strains.

Mitosis. A sequence of cellular events that culminates in the division of a eukaryotic nucleus into two genetically similar or identical nuclei whose ploidy is the same as that of the parent nucleus. Mitosis occurs during asexual cell division.

Mitospore. A uninucleate, haploid or diploid spore arising by mitosis.

Mitosporic fungi. See Deuteromycotina.

MLO. Mycoplasma-like organism. See phytoplasma.

Mold. A downy fungal growth on a substratum, usually consisting of mycelium of a Hyphomycete or a Zygomycete.

Mollicute. A proposed trivial name for any member of the class Mollicutes. The use of this name could permit "mycoplasmas" to be used specifically for members of the genus Mycoplasma.

Molt. To cast off the cuticle.

Monocyclic. Of a disease or pathogen: Producing one generation of inoculum and one cycle of infection during a single growing season. (See polycyclic.)

Monodelphic. Of nematodes: Possessing one genital tube or ovary.

Monoecious. Having male and female reproductive organs on a single thallus.

Monogenic resistance. Resistance determined by a single gene.

Monogenic. Of nematodes: Producing offspring of only one sex.

Monokaryotic. Having one nucleus per cell.

Monophialide. See conidiophore.

Monotype. The sole species of a newly proposed genus.

Morphologic. Pertaining to form.

Mosaic. A common symptom induced in leaves by many plant virus infections in which there is a pattern of dark green, light green and sometimes chlorotic areas. This pattern is often associated with the distribution of veins in the leaf. In monocotyledonous leaves it shows as stripes.

Mottle. A diffuse form of the mosaic symptom in plant leaves in which the dark and light green are less sharply defined. This term is frequently used interchangeably with mosaic.

MRNA. See messenger RNA.

Mucronate. In nematodes: Ending in a sharp point.

Mulch. A protective covering that is spread on the ground around plants to inhibit evaporation and weed growth, control soil temperature, enrich the soil, or prevent the dispersal of pathogens. It may be organic material such as leaves, peat, or wood chips, or inorganic material such as plastic sheeting.

Multicomponent virus. A virus in which the genome needed for full infection is divided between two or more particles (e.g., cowpea mosaic virus, brome mosaic virus, cucumber mosaic virus).

Multiline. A plant cultivar made up of a mixture of isolines differing in their genes for resistance to a particular pathogen. (Also **multiline cultivar**.)

Multiseptate. Having more than one septum.

Mummy. A dried, shrivelled fruit colonized by a fungus.

Muriform. Having bricklike cells in a wall with both longitudinal and transverse septa.

Mushroom. A fleshy fruiting body of a fungus, especially of a basidiomycete of the family Agaricaceae.

Mutant. Of an organism, population, gene, chromosome, etc.: Differing from the corresponding wild type by changes in one or more loci.

Mutation. A stable, heritable change in the nucleotide sequence of a genetic nucleic acid (DNA, or RNA in viruses, viroids, etc) typically resulting in the generation of a new allele and a new phenotype.

Mutualism. See symbiosis.

Mycelium. A mass of hyphae, often used to denote all hyphae comprising a thallus.

Mycology. The study of fungi.

Mycoparasite. A fungus parasitic on other fungi.

Mycoparasitism. One fungus living on another.

Mycophagous. Feeding on fungi.

Mycoplasma. A genus of cell wall-less, sterol-requiring, catalase-negative bacteria (family Mycoplasmataceae) occurring as parasites and pathogens.

Mycoplasma. A wall-less prokaryotic microorganism of the class Mollicutes.

Mycoplasma-like organism. See phytoplasma.

Mycorrhiza. A specialized root structure resulting from a symbiotic relationship between a fungus and a higher plant.

Mycosis. Disease in animals caused by a fungus.

Mycotoxicosis. Any disease of man or animals resulting from the ingestion of mycotoxins.

Mycotoxin. A toxin produced by a fungus. The term is usually reserved for fungal metabolites that are toxic to man and/or animals and are produced by molds growing on foodstuffs (e.g., aflatoxins, ergot alkaloids).

Mycotrophic. Refers to green plants having mycorrhizae.

Mycovirus. A virus that replicates in cells of fungi.

Myxamoeba. A naked cell capable of amoeboid movement; characteristic of the vegetative phase of myxomycetes and such Plasmodiophoromycetes as *Plasmodiophora brassicae.*

Myxomycetes. See **Myxomycota.**

Myxomycota. The slime molds, a class of fungi characterized by amoeboid vegetative protoplasts, plasmodia, and by brightly colored spore bearing capillitia.

N

Necrosis. Localized death of cells or tissues.

Necrotic. Dead.

Necrotroph. 1. An organism that kills part or all of another organism before deriving nutrients from it (usually applied to plant pathogens). 2. An organism that derives nutrients from dead plant or animal tissues, whether or not it is responsible for the death of those tissues.

Nematicide. A chemical compound or physical agent that kills nematodes.

Nematode. More or less elongate, spindle-shaped, worm-like animals ranging in size from less than a millimeter to several meters in length, living as saprophytes in soil or water or as parasites of plants or animals.

Neotype. A specimen selected as the type subsequent to the original description in cases in which the primary types are definitely known to have been destroyed.

Nepovirus. (Siglum of nematode polyhedral virus). Member of a group of multicomponent plant viruses with two isometric particles containing two species of linear RNA, transmitted mechanically and by soil-inhabiting nematodes.

Nerve ring. The center of the nervous system of nematodes that encircles the esophagus; composed largely of nerve fibers and associated ganglia.

Nomenclature. A system of names, or naming, as applied to the subjects or study in any art or science, especially in botany and zoology.

Noncirculative transmission. Virus transmission characterized by a very short period of acquisition of the virus by a vector (e.g., an aphid), no latent period before the vector can transmit the virus, and a short period of retention by the vector after acquisition. (Also termed **nonpresistent transmission**.)

Nonseptate. Lacking cross-walls.

Northern blot. An RNA blot. This term originated as lab jargon; not a generally accepted term.

Nuclease. Any enzyme that can cleave the sugar-phosphate backbone of a nucleic acid.

Nucleoprotein. A compound of nucleic acid and protein.

Nutrient broth. A liquid basal medium.

O

Obligate. Restricted to a particular set of environmental conditions, without which an organism cannot survive. (e.g., an obligate parasite can survive only by parasitizing another organism.)

Obligate anaerobe. An organism that can grow only under anaerobic conditions.

Obligate parasite. An organism that is incapable of living as a saprophyte and must live as a parasite.

Oblong. (Of spores) longer than broad (about twice as long or somewhat less), with sides nearly parallel and with ends more or less flattened.

Obovate. Egg-shaped, with the wide end outward.

Obovoid. Egg-shaped, with the narrow end outward.

Obtuse. (Of pileus, cystidia, spores) rounded or blunt.

Odontostylet. See stylet. Synonymous with onchiostylet.

Oedema. Intumescence or blister formation because of an increase in intercellular water. (Also **edema**.)

Onchiostylet. In nematodes: A stylet developed from a special cell in the anterior part of the esophagus from which it moves into place during each molt.

Ontogeny. Development of the individual.

Oocyst. Synonymous with oogonium.

Oocyte. Female germ cell.

Oogamy. A type of heterogamy in which plasmogamy takes place between a large nonmotile egg and a small motile male gamete or cytoplasm from an antheridium.

Oogonium. A female gametangium that contains one or more discrete gametes.

Oomycete. A member of the Oomycetes.

Oomycetes. A class of aquatic and terrestrial fungi (subdivision Mastigomycotina) that typically produce oogonia and zoosporangia in which form zoospores having one anteriorly-directed tinsel flagellum and one posteriorly-directed whiplash flagellum.

Oosphere. A large, naked, nonmotile, usually spherical, female gamete.

Oospore. A thick-walled spore that develops from an oosphere through plasmogamy or parthenogenesis.

Operculate. Of an ascus or sporangium, opening by a subcircular apical lid to discharge spores, as in asci of the Pezizales.

Operculum. A flap or lid-like covering over the opening of an ascus or sporangium.

Opisthodelphic. Of nematodes: Having the uterus (or uteri) directed posteriorly.

Ostiole. 1. A neck-like structure in an ascocarp, lined with pariphyses, and terminating in a pore. 2. The opening of a pycnidium.

Ostiolum. See ostiole.

Ovary. Female sexual gland in which the ova, or eggs, are formed.

Oviduct. A short, usually tubular, thick-walled part of the female reproductive system between the ovary and spermatheca.

Oviparous. Producing eggs that hatch after expulsion from the body.

Ovoid. Egg-shaped.

Ovoviviparous. Producing eggs that hatch within the body.

P

Page. Polyacrylamide gel electrophoresis.

Papilla. A hump or swelling.

Papillate. Bearing a papilla.

Paraphysis. Sterile, elongated cell that may occur in the hymenium, intermixed with asci or basidia, elongating apically and having a free apex.

Parasexual cycle. A sequence involving heterokaryon formation, diploidization, and haploidization, often resulting in the formation of recombinant nuclei. Unlike the sexual cycle, the parasexual cycle can occur at any point or continuously throughout the life cycle.

Parasite. An organism living in or on another living organism (host) from which it extracts nutrients.

Parasitic. Having the characteristics of a parasite.

Paratype. A specimen other than the holotype and its isotypes that the author cited at the time of publication of the original description.

Parenchyma. A tissue composed of living, thin-walled cells that can continue to divide even when mature; parenchyma cells usually leave intercellular spaces between them.

Parthenogenesis. Process of reproduction by the development of an unfertilized egg.

Parthenogenic. Pertaining to parthenogenesis.

Pathogen. An agent (biotic or abiotic) that causes plant disease.

Pathogenesis. That portion of the life cycle of a pathogen during which it becomes, and continues to be, associated with its suscept.

Pathogenic. Having the characteristics of a pathogen.

Pathogenicity. The capability of a pathogen to cause disease.

Pathology. 1. The study of disease. 2. The abnormal condition that constitutes disease.

Pathotype. An infrasubspecific classification of a pathogen distinguished from others of the species by its pathogenicity on a specific host(s).

Pathovar. In bacteria: An infrasubspecific group that can infect only plants within a certain genus or species. See pathotype.

PCR. See polymerase chain reaction.

Pellet. The material concentrated at the bottom of a centrifuge tube after centrifugation.

Peloderan. In nematodes: Caudal alae that meet posterior to the tail tip.

Penetration peg. In some plant parasitic fungi: The peg-like hypha emerging from an appressorium that penetrates the epidermal cell wall.

Perfect state. The state of a fungus characterized by sexual spores.

Peridermium. A blister-like aecium as in the form genus *Peridermium.*

Peridium. A wall or membrane of sterile cells around a fruiting body (e.g., around a sporangium or delimiting an aecium).

Perineal pattern. Fingerprint-like pattern formed by cuticular striae surrounding the vulva and anus of the mature *Meloidogyne* female.

Periphysis. Short, hair-like filaments that line the canal of the ostiole in some Pyrenomycetes.

Perithecioid. Like a perithecium.

Perithecium. A closed ascocarp with a pore at the top, a true ostiole, and a wall of its own.

Peritrichous. Of bacterial flagella: Distributed more or less uniformly over the cell surface.

Peronosporales. Specialized forms of the Oomycetes, including aquatic and terrestrial species; many species in this order are plant pathogens (damping-off fungi, downy mildews, and white rusts); unlike the true fungi, they lack chitin in their cell walls.

Persistent transmission. See circulative transmission.

Phage. A general term used for viruses isolated from prokaryotes including bacteria, blue-green algae (cyanobacteria) and mollicutes (phytoplasma and spiroplasma). The viruses from these different host groups are termed bacteriophages, cyanophages and mycoplasmaphages, respectively.

Phasmid. In nematodes: A pore-like structure located in the lateral field of the posterior region of nematodes belonging to the class Secernentea. Function is believed to be sensory. Sometimes called precaudal glands.

Phenotype. The observable characteristics of an organism, either in total or with respect to one or more particular named characteristics.

Phloem. Food-conducting tissue, consisting of sieve tubes, companion cells, phloem parenchyma, and fibers.

Phragmobasidium. A basidium that is divided into more than one cell by transverse or longitudinal septa.

Phragmospore. A spore having two to many transverse septa.

Phragmosporous. Having transversely multiseptate spores.

Phyllody. A change of floral petals (leaves) to foliage leaves.

Phylloplane. The surface(s) of a leaf.

Physiologic specialization. The existence of a number of races or forms of one species of pathogen based on their pathogenicity to different cultivars of a host.

Physiological race. A subdivision of a species of pathogen, particularly fungi, distinguished from other members of the species by specialization for pathogenicity to different cultivars of a host.

Phytoalexin. A low molecular weight, antimicrobial compound synthesized by and accumulating in higher plants exposed to certain microorganisms (pathogenic and nonpathogenic).

Phytopathogenic. Of microorganisms: Capable of initiating disease in plants.

Phytoplasma. A prokaryotic, plant parasitic microorganism resembling a mycoplasma but not yet isolable in pure culture or characterized taxonomically.

Phytotoxic. Toxic to plants.

Phytotoxin. 1. A toxin produced by a microorganism and active against a plant or against plant cells/tissues. 2. A toxin produced by a plant.

Pileate. Possessing a cap or pileus.

Pileus. The expanded caplike portion of some basidiocarps or ascocarps that supports the hymenium.

Plasmalemma. The cytoplasmic membrane found on the outside of the protoplast adjacent to the cell wall.

Plasmid. In many types of prokaryotic and eukaryotic cell: a linear or covalently closed circular molecule of DNA, (distinct from chromosomal DNA, mtDNA, ctDNA, or kDNA and commonly dispensable to the cell), that can replicate autonomously (i.e., independently of other replicons).

Plasmodesma. A fine protoplasmic thread connecting two protoplasts and passing through the wall separating the two protoplasts.

Plasmodium. A multinucleated, usually naked (i.e., bounded only by a plasma membrane) mass of protoplasm that is usually motile and variable in size and form.

Plasmogamy. The fusion of two protoplasts.

Plasmolysis. The shrinking and separation of the cytoplasm from the cell wall due to exosmosis of water from the protoplast.

Plectomycete. A member of the Plectomycetes.

Plectomycetes. In general, a group of primitive or reduced ascomycetous forms that have an angiocarpous fructification without an ostiole, the entire interior of which is irregularly penetrated by ascogenous hyphae, with the result that the generally spherical asci, without accompanying paraphyses or other threads, lie scattered irregularly in a pseudoparenchymatous tissue composed of the ascogenous hyphae.

Pleomorphic. Exhibiting pleomorphism.

Pleomorphism. 1. In fungi: Having more than one independent form or spore stage in the life cycle. 2. In general: An inherent variability in size and shape (e.g., among the cells in a pure culture or clone of a given organism).

Plerome. The plant tissues inside the cortex.

Plesionecrosis A symptom exhibited by tissues not yet dead but in the process of dying (e.g., wilting).

Ploidy. The number of (complete) sets of chromosomes in a cell.

Polar. At one end or pole of the cell (e.g., a flagellum, spore inclusion, germ tube, etc.).

Polycyclic. Of a disease or pathogen: Producing many generations of inoculum and many cycles of infection during a single growing season. (See monocyclic.)

Polyetic. Of plant disease epidemics: Continuing from one growing season to the next.

Polygenic. A character controlled by many genes.

Polymerase chain reaction. The selective amplification of DNA by repeated cycles of (a) heat denaturation of the DNA, (b) annealing of two oligonucleotide primers that flank the DNA segment to be amplified and (c) the extension of the annealed primers with the heat insensitive *Taq* DNA polymerase.

Polymorphism. Pleomorphism.

Polynucleate. Having more than one nucleus per cell.

Polypore. A member of the Polyporaceae; the hymenium forms tubes in the basidiocarp.

Poroconidium. See porospore.

Porospore. A conidium produced by an extension of the inner wall of the conidiogenous cell and extrusion through a pore in the wall of the conidiophore.

Potexvirus. (Siglum of potato virus X.) Member of a group of plant viruses that infect a wide range of hosts, including monocots and dicots; individual members infect only a narrow host range, typically causing mosaic and ringspot symptoms. Type member: potato virus X (PVX).

Potyvirus. (Siglum of potato virus Y). Member of a large group of plant viruses with flexuous particles containing a single molecule of linear RNA, most of which are transmitted by aphids in a noncirculative manner.

Predisposition. An increase in susceptibility resulting from the influence of environment on the suscept.

Primary cycle. Of plant disease: the first infection cycle to begin in a given season; usually occurring only once per season.

Primary infection. The first infection of a plant by a pathogen emerging from a dormant stage in its life cycle (overwintering or oversummering).

Primary inoculum. The overwintering or oversummering pathogen or its propagules that cause primary infection.

Probasidium. The cell in which karyogamy occurs in the basidiomycetes.

Probe. A specific sequence of DNA or RNA used to detect complementary sequences by hybridization.

Procorpus. In nematodes: Cylindrical portion of the corpus anterior to the metacorpus.

Prodelphic. In nematodes: Having uteri parallel and anteriorly directed at the origin.

Prolepsis. A hyperplastic symptom of disease in which organs appear before the natural time.

Proliferation. A rapid and repeated production of new cells, tissues, or organs; specifically, a hyperplastic symptom of plant disease in which organs continue to develop after they have reached the point beyond which they normally do not grow.

Promoter. A region of DNA, usually upstream of a coding sequence, that binds RNA polymerase and directs the enzyme to the correct transcriptional start site.

Promycelium. The short hypha bearing sporidia produced by the teliospore; the basidium.

Propagative virus. A circulative virus that replicates in its insect vector. Such a virus is said to be propagatively transmitted (e.g., potato yellow dwarf virus).

Propagule. Any disseminative unit of an organism (e.g., a spore, a mycelial fragment a sclerotium).

Protease. A generic term for an enzyme that cleaves a polypeptide chain.

Protectant. Any chemical agent that interacts with a pathogen on the plant surface to inhibit infection before it takes place. Non systemic.

Protection. A principle of plant disease control in which a barrier is placed between suscept and pathogen (e.g., the use of protective chemical dusts or sprays).

Protoplast. A plant cell from which the cell wall has been removed.

Prototroph. A strain of microorganism whose nutritional requirements do not exceed those of the corresponding wild-type strain.

Pseudocoel. In nematodes: Body cavity containing a fluid in which the various internal organs are suspended.

Pseudoparaphysis. A sterile thread that grows downward in the cavity of some ascocarps, usually becoming attached at the bottom.

Pseudothecium. An ascostroma resembling a flask-shaped perithecium.

Punctate. Having surface dot(s), pore(s), etc.

Pustule. Small blister-like elevation of the leaf epidermis created as spores emerge from underneath and push outward.

Pv. Pathovar.

Pycnidiospore. A conidium formed in a pycnidium.

Pycnidium. A closed sporocarp, usually opening by a pore, that contains a cavity bearing conidia.

Pycniospore. A spore (spermatium) borne in a pycnium in the Uredinales.

Pycnium. In the Uredinales, stage 0, consisting of the male fertilizing elements (pycniospores) and female elements, the flexuous hyphae.

Pycnospore. An obsolete term for a pycnidiospore or a pycniospore.

Pygmism. The state of being dwarfed or reduced in size.

Pyrenomycete. One of the Pyrenomycetes.

Pyrenomycetes. Class of Ascomycotina, traditionally based on taxa with perithecioid ascomata that are ascohymenial in ontogeny and have unitunicate asci, often with an apical annulus.

Pyriform. Pear-shaped.

Q

Quarantine. Legal restriction of the movement of plant pests (or the products that may be harboring them) into areas where they do not occur.

Quiescence. That period of the prepenetration stage during which a pathogen may be inactive because environmental conditions are unfavorable for its growth.

R

Race. A subspecies group of pathogens that infect a given set of plant varieties.

Rachis. In fungi: A conidiophore elongating to one side of a terminally produced spore, often resulting in a zig-zag-shaped structure.

Range. Of a plant pathogen: The geographical region or regions in which it is known to occur.

Recombinant DNA. DNA molecules in which sequences, not normally contiguous, have been placed next to each other by *in vitro* methods.

Rectum. In nematodes: Posterior gut of the female. A narrow, dorsoventrally flattened tube that is lined with cuticle and separated from the intestine by a sphincter muscle.

Reflexed. Bent back.

REMI (Restriction enzyme mediated integration). A method of transformation that generates tagged mutations.

Reniform. Kidney-shaped.

Replicon. Any DNA sequence or molecule that possesses a replication origin and is therefore potentially capable of being replicated in a suitable cell.

Resistance. The ability of an organism to exclude or overcome, completely or in some degree, the effect of a pathogen or other damaging factor.

Resistant. Possessing resitance.

Response. The change produced in an organism by a stimulus.

Resting spore. A thick-walled spore, particularly one formed by a sexual process, germinating only after an extended period of dormancy (e.g., an overwintering teliospore).

Restriction endonuclease. An endonuclease that binds to double-stranded DNA at a specific nucleotide sequence and then, if both strands of the DNA lack appropriate modification at that sequence, cleaves the DNA either at the recognition sequence or at another site in the DNA molecule.

Reticulate. Having net-like markings.

Retrorse. In a backward or downward direction.

Revolute. Of the margin of the pileus: rolled back or up.

RFLP (Restriction fragment length polymorphism). Inherited differences in sites for restriction enzymes (e.g., caused by base changes in the target site) that result in differences in the lengths of the fragments produced by cleavage with the relevant restriction enzyme. RFLPs are used for genetic mapping to link the genome directly to a conventional genetic marker.

Rhabdions. In nematodes: Plates in the cuticular lining of the stoma that make up the walls of the various divisions of the stoma.

Rhizoid. A root-like structure forming part of the thallus in certain algae and fungi; it may anchor the organism to the substratum and/or act as an absorptive organ.

Rhizomorph. A macroscopic, typically rope-like strand of compacted tissue formed by certain higher fungi. Rhizomorphs often are enduring structures that can remain dormant under adverse conditions.

Rhizomycelium. Branching, anucleate or sparsely nucleate, rhizoidal filaments of variable width forming part of the thallus in some fungi.

Rhizoplane. The root surface.

Rhizosphere. An environment regarded, variously, as (a) that region of the soil modified as a result of the uptake and deposition of substances by a growing root, (b) the root itself, together with that volume of soil which it influences, (c) the root surface together with that region of the surrounding soil in which the microbial population is affected by the presence of a root.

Rickettsiae. Microorganisms similar to bacteria in most respects but generally capable of multiplying only inside living host cells; parasitic or symbiotic.

Ringspot. A type of local lesion consisting of single or concentric rings of discoloration or necrosis, the regions between the concentric rings being green. The center of the lesion may be chlorotic or necrotic.

RNA blotting. A technique for transferring RNA from an agarose gel to a nitrocellulose filter on which it can be hybridized to a complementary DNA.

Roestelium. In the Uredinales an aecium with a cornute peridium, thin at the sides, usually rupturing by longitudinal slits, and made up of characteristically marked and imbricated cells. The name is taken from the form-genus *Roestelia*.

Rogue. A variation from the standard varietal type; also, to remove such undesirable plants (especially those infected with viruses) from the growing crop.

Roguing. The removal of diseased plants from a crop in order to prevent the spread of the disease.

Rosette. An abnormal condition in which the leaves form a radial cluster on the stem.

Rot. The softening, discoloration, and often disintegration of a succulent plant tissue as a result of fungal or bacterial infection.

Roundworm. Nematode.

Rugose. Wrinkled.

Russet. Brownish, roughened areas on the skin of fruit as a result of cork formation.

Rust. 1. Fungus of the class Urediniomycetes. 2. Any of various plant diseases caused by members of the Urediniomycetes or by species of *Albugo*. The diseases are called "rusts" because many of the causal agents form rust-colored spores on affected plants.

S

Saccate. Pouch- or sac-like.

Saltation. A mutation occurring in the asexual state of fungal growth, especially one occurring in culture.

Sanitation. Principle of plant disease control involving removal and burning of infected plant parts and decontamination of tools, equipment, hands, etc.

Saprobe. An organism that obtains its nutrients from non-living organic matter (commonly dead and decaying plant or animal matter) by absorbing soluble organic compounds. (Also **saprotroph**.)

Saprogenesis. Survival; that phase of the life cycle of a pathogen during which it is not actively causing disease in a living suscept.

Saprophyte. See saprobe.

Saprotroph. See saprobe.

Sarcody. A hyperplastic symptom in which swellings occur above and below portions of organs that are tightly encircled.

Satellite virus. A defective virus requiring a helper virus to provide functions necessary for replication. It may code for its own coat protein or various other products.

Scab. Any of a wide range of unrelated plant diseases having a roughened, crustlike diseased area on the surface of a plant organ (e.g., apple scab, potato scab, wheat scab).

Scabrous. Rough with short, rigid projections.

Scald. A necrotic condition in which tissue is usually bleached and has the appearance of having been exposed to high temperatures.

Sclerotium. Hard, resistant, multicellular resting body, usually with a differentiated cortex and medulla, that under favorable conditions can germinate to produce mycelium or sexual or asexual fruiting bodies.

Sclerotized. In nematodes: Hardened refractive regions.

Scolecospore. A very long, thin spore (with a length/width ratio more than 15:1).

Scolecosporous. Having long, thin (filiform) spores.

Scorch. "Burning" of leaf margins as a result of infection or unfavorable environmental conditions.

Scutellum. In nematodes: An enlarged, shield-like phasmid.

Secondary cycle. Of plant disease: any cycle initiated by inoculum generated during the same season.

Secondary infection. Any infection caused by inoculum produced as a result of a primary or a subsequent infection; an infection caused by secondary inoculum.

Secondary inoculum. Inoculum produced by infections that took place during the same growing season.

Secondary organism. An organism that multiplies in already diseased tissue but is not the primary pathogen.

Secondary rot. Rot caused by a secondary organism.

Secondary symptom. A symptom of virus infection appearing after the first (primary) symptoms.

Sedentary. Staying in one place; stationary.

Senescence. Decline or degeneration, as with maturation, age, or disease stress.

Senescent. Aged, degenerate.

Sensu lato. In a broad sense.

Sensu stricto. In a narrow sense.

Septate. Having cross walls.

Septum. A cross wall in a hypha or spore.

Sequence. The order of nucleotides in RNA or DNA or of amino acids in a polypeptide.

Sequencing. Determining a sequence of a nucleic acid or protein.

Serology. Branch of science dealing with properties and reactions of sera, particularly the use of antibodies in the sera to examine the properties of antigens.

Serotype. A subdivision of virus strains distinguished by protein or a protein component that determines its antigenic specificity.

Serum. The fluid fraction of coagulated (clotted) blood.

Seta. 1. In nematodes: Elongated cuticular structures articulating with the cuticle; in general, tactile sensory organs usually located around the oral openings. 2. In fungi: A bristle-like structure in some types of fruiting bodies.

Setose. Bristly; beset with bristles.

Sexual dimorphism. A pronounced difference in the morphologies of the two sexes within a species.

Shock symptoms. The severe, often necrotic symptoms produced on the first new growth following infection with some viruses. Also called **acute symptoms**.

Shot hole. A symptom in which small, diseased fragments of leaves fall off, leaving small holes in their place.

Sieve plate. Perforated wall area between two phloem sieve cells through which they are connected.

Sieve tube. A series of phloem cells forming a long cellular tube through which food materials are transported.

Sigmoid. Doubly curved in opposite directions, like the Greek letter sigma.

Sign. A visible manifestation of a causal agent of plant disease (e.g., fungal spores or other fungal structures, bacterial ooze).

Slime mold. A member of a category of eukaryotic organisms that typically have some fungal-like attributes and some animal-like attributes.

Smut spore. A dark, thick-walled resting spore of a smut fungus; may germinate to produce a promycelium; often improperly termed a chlamydospore.

Smut. Any of a number of plant diseases caused by the smut fungi (Ustilaginales); characterized by masses of dark, powdery, and sometimes odorous spores (e.g., stinking smut of wheat, common smut of maize).

Somaclonal variation. Variability in clones generated from a single mother plant, leaf, etc. by tissue culture.

Somatic cell hybridization. Production of hybrid cells by fusion of two protoplasts with different genetic makeup.

Sooty mold. A fungus of the family Capnodiaceae and of certain other families of the order Dothideales. The organisms grow epiphytically, utilizing honeydew, and form dark, spongy, hyphal mats on the surfaces of certain plants.

Sorus. A cluster or mass of spores or sporangia.

Southern blotting. Procedure for transferring denatured DNA from an agarose gel to a nitrocellulose filter where it can be hybridized with a complementary nucleic acid.

Spear. See stylet.

Species epithet. (Bot.) The second word of a species name (e.g., *graminis* in the species *Puccinia graminis*).

Species name. (Bot.) A Latin name consisting of two words, the generic name and the species epithet (e.g., *Puccinia graminis*).

Species. The basic category of biological classification, displaying a high degree of mutual similarity determined by a consensus of informed opinion; a subcategory of genus.

Spermagonium. In certain fungi: a structure within which male reproductive cells (spermatia) are formed. In rust fungi, a spermagonium is called a pycnium.

Spermatheca. In nematodes: An enlarged portion of the female gonad between the oviduct and the uterus functioning in the storage of the sperm.

Spermatium. 1. A non-motile male reproductive cell that can function in spermatization. 2. The male gamete of the rust fungi. See pycniospore.

Spermatization. In certain higher fungi: the union of a spermatium with a female reproductive structure.

Spermatocyte. In nematodes: A cell giving rise to spermatozoa or spermatozooids.

Spicate. Having the form of a spike.

Spicule. Male copulatory organ. Sometimes called spiculum.

Spiroplasma. A member of a group of pleomorphic, wall-less prokaryotes occurring as epiphytes or as intracellular or extracellular parasites or pathogens in a range of invertebrates and plants.

Sporangiophore. A modified hypha that supports the sporangium.

Sporangiospore. An asexual spore produced within a sporangium.

Sporangium. A sac that bears endogenous, asexual spores (sporangiospores).

Spore. A discrete sexual or asexual reproductive unit, usually enclosed by a rigid wall, capable of being disseminated.

Sporidiole. A little spore.

Sporidiolum. See sporidiole.

Sporidium. 1. A basidiospore formed by the rust or smut fungi. 2. In smut fungi: a spore formed in germination by repetition.

Sporocarp. A fruit body that produces spores.

Sporodochium. A cluster of conidiophores arising from a stroma or mass of hyphae.

Sporophore. A spore-producing or spore-bearing structure such as a conidiophore, ascocarp, or basidiocarp.

Sporulate. To produce spores.

Sporulation. The process of producing spores.

Spot. A symptom of disease characterized by a limited necrotic area, as on leaves, flowers, and stems.

Spreader. A substance added to fungicide or bactericide preparations to improve contact between the spray and the sprayed surface; a surfactant.

Squamous. Covered with or consisting of scales.

Squamule. A small scale or lobe.

Staurospore. A non-septate or septate spore with more than one axis.

Staurosporous. Possessing staurospores.

Stem-pitting. A symptom of some viral diseases characterized by depressions on the stem of the plant.

Sterigma. A spike-like structure that supports a basidiospore on the basidium.

Sterile fungus. A fungus that is not known to produce any kind of spores.

Sterile. 1. Unable to reproduce sexually. 2. To be free from living microorganisms.

Sterilization. The elimination of pathogens and other living organisms from soil, containers, etc. by means of heat, chemicals, or radiation.

Sterilized. Free from living microorganisms.

Sticker. Added to fungicide or bactericide preparations to improve the adhesion of the spray to the sprayed surface.

Stipe. The stalk-like portion of some larger ascocarps or basidiocarps; any spore-bearing stalk.

Stoma. 1. In plants: Aperture in the epidermis of a leaf, stem, or fruit, bound by two guard cells and functioning in gas exchange. 2. In nematodes: Buccal capsule.

Stomatostylet. See stylet.

Strain. A sub-species group of organisms distinguishable from the rest of the species by a heritable characteristic that the individuals in the group have in common.

Striae. In nematodes: Superficial grooves or clefts on the cuticle; when present, striae may be seen encircling lips or body.

Striate. Marked with delicate lines, grooves, or ridges.

Stroma. A compact mass of vegetative tissue, sometimes intermixed with host tissue, often bearing sporocarps either within or upon its surface.

Stylet knob. One of the (usually three) basal protuberances of the stylet.

Stylet. In nematodes: Hollow protrusible spear used to puncture plants or animal prey.

Stylospore. A spore borne on a filament or hypha.

Suberized. Of cell walls: Hardened by their conversion to cork (suberin).

Subsp. Subspecies.

Subspecies. An infraspecific population defined on the basis of one or more characters (morphologic for most organisms) that distinguish its members from typical representatives of the species.

Substrate. 1. The material or substance on which a microorganism feeds and develops. 2. a substance acted upon by an enzyme.

Superinfection. Attempt to infect a host with a second virus, usually a different strain of the first infecting virus.

Supernatant. The material remaining above the pellet after centrifugation of a suspension.

Supplements. In nematodes: Preanal genital papillae on the ventral side of males; derived from cuticle, but may be provided with glands. Function during copulation. Sometimes called supplementary organs.

Suppression. A hypoplastic symptom characterized by the failure of plant organs or substances to develop.

Suppressive soil. A soil in which certain disease(s) fail to develop because of the presence in the soil of microorganisms antagonistic to the pathogen.

Suscept. Any plant that can be attacked by a given pathogen; a host.

Susceptibility. The inability of a plant to resist the effect of a pathogen or other damaging factor.

Susceptible. Lacking the inherent ability to resist disease or attack by a given pathogen; not immune.

Suspensor. A specialized hyphal tip that supports a gametangium and eventually a zygosporangium (in the Mucorales).

Swarmspore. Zoospore.

Symbiont. One member of a symbiotic relationship.

Symbiosis. A mutually beneficial association of two or more different kinds of organisms.

Symbiote. Symbiont.

Symptom. A visible abnormality in a plant that results from disease.

Symptomatology. The study of symptoms of disease and signs of pathogens for the purpose of diagnosis.

Symptomless carrier. A plant that, although infected with a pathogen (usually a virus), produces no obvious symptoms.

Synanamorph. Any one of the two or more anamorphs that are formed by the same fungus.

Syncytium. A multinucleate cell.

Synergism. The concurrent parasitism of a host by two pathogens in which the symptoms or other effects produced are of greater magnitude than the sum of the effects of each pathogen acting alone.

Synnema. A fascicle of conidiophores, usually upright; a coremium.

Syntype. One of a number of specimens of equal nomenclatural rank that formed all or part of the material the original author had in cases in which the author did not designate or indicate a holotype.

Systemic infection. In virology, an infection resulting from the spread of virus from the site of infection to all or most cells of an organism.

Systemic. Of a chemical or a pathogen: Spreading internally throughout the plant body.

T

Tail. In nematodes: The portion of the body between the anus and the posterior terminus.

Taxon. A taxonomic group of any rank.

Telamon. In nematodes: Rigid, sclerotized portion of the cloacal wall that apparently guides the spicules from the spicular pouch into the cloaca.

Teleomorph. The stage characterized by the production of asci/ascospores, basidia/basidiospores, teliospores, or other basidium-bearing organs.

Teleutosorus. An old term for telium.

Teleutospore. See teliospore.

Teliospore. A usually thick-walled, usually resting spore, which is the site of karyogamy and produces the basidium (in the Uredinales and Ustilaginales).

Telium. The final sorus (stage III) produced in the life cycle of the Uredinales and producing teliospores.

Tessellate. In nematodes: Checkered; a type of cuticular pattern in which the longitudinal ridges are broken by transverse striations into rows of squares.

Testis. A male reproductive organ in which spermatozoa are produced.

Texture. The arrangement of the components of the different tissues, as compact, loose, etc.

Thallic. One of two basic kinds of conidiogenesis; the conidial initial enlarges *after* it has been delimited by one or more septa. The conidium is differentiated from a *whole* cell. (See blastic.)

Thallospore. A conidium that has no conidiophore or is not separate from the hypha or conidiophore that produced it.

Thallus. Any simple vegetative plant body that lacks roots, stems and leaves.

Therapy. Principle of plant disease control marked by the cure of disease, as with heat or systemic chemicals.

Threadworm. Nematode.

Tissue. A group of cells of similar structure which performs a special function.

Titillae. In nematodes: Small projections on either side of the distal end of the gubernaculum.

Toadstool. Mushroom.

Tobamovirus. (Siglum of tobacco mosaic virus). Member of a group of plant viruses with rigid, rod-shaped particles containing one molecule of linear RNA, easily sap-transmitted and transmitted in nature by contact and (in the case of some viruses in this group) in seed.

Tolerance. 1. The ability of a plant to sustain the effects of a disease without dying or suffering serious injury or crop loss. 2. The amount of toxic residue allowable in or on edible plant parts under the law.

Tombusvirus. (Siglum of tomato bushy stunt virus). Member of a group of plant viruses with isometric (icosahedral) particles containing one molecule of linear RNA, readily sap-transmitted and also transmitted through soil.

Topotype. A specimen collected at the type locality.

Tospovirus. (Siglum of tomato spotted wilt virus). Member of a small group of plant viruses with spherical particles containing three RNA species, transmitted in nature by thrips in a persistent manner.

Toxicity. The capacity of a compound to produce injury or death.

Toxin. A compound produced by a microorganism and being toxic to a plant or animal.

Trama. The sterile tissue of a basidiocarp.

Transduction. The virus-mediated transfer of host DNA (chromosomal or plasmid) from one host cell (the donor) to another (the recipient). Transduction was first observed in bacteriophage/bacterium systems, but has since also been found to be mediated by certain viruses infecting eukaryotic cells.

Transfection. The successful virus-infection of cells following their inoculation with viral nucleic acid.

Transformant. A cell or organism that has undergone genetic transformation.

Transformation. A process in which exogenous DNA is taken up by a (recipient) cell or protoplast, in which it may be incorporated into the chromosome (or, e.g., into a plasmid) by homologous recombination or converted into an autonomous replicon. The DNA (transforming or donor DNA) may be a fragment of chromosomal DNA from a related strain, a plasmid, or a viral genome.

Translocation. Transfer of nutrients or virus through the plant.

Transmission. The transfer of a pathogen from one plant to another, or from one plant organ to another.

Transpiration. The loss of water vapor from the surface of leaves and other aboveground parts of plants.

Transposon. A discrete piece of DNA that can insert itself into other DNA sequences within the cell. The ends of the transposon DNA are usually inverted repeats.

Tretic. Of conidiogenesis: The sort of blastic conidiogenesis in which each conidium is delimited by an extension of the inner wall of the conidiogenous cell. Tretoconidia are solitary or in acropetal chains.

Trichogyne. In some algae, lichens, and fungi, a projection from the female sex organ that receives the male gamete or nuclei before fertilization (karyogamy).

Trifurcate. Bearing three branches or forks.

Triradiate. Having three radiating arms or branches.

Truncate. Having the end squared off or even.

Tumefaction. A plant tumor or gall.

Tumor. An uncontrolled growth of tissue or tissues.

Tylosis. A balloon-like outgrowth from a xylem parenchyma cell that expands into and blocks the lumen of a xylem vessel or a tracheid.

Tymovirus. (Siglum of turnip yellow mosaic virus). Member of a group of plant viruses with isometric (icosahedral) particles containing a single molecule of linear RNA, easily transmitted mechanically and transmitted in nature by beetles.

Type. An object that serves as the basis for the name of a taxon.

U

Umbilicate. Of the pileus: Having a central navel-like depression, sunken in the center, somewhat funnel-shaped.

Umbo. Of the pileus: A raised, conical to convex knob or mound on the center.

Umbonate. Of the pileus: provided with an umbo or boss.

Uninucleate. Having one nucleus per cell.

Unipolar. At one end only.

Uniseptate. Having one septum.

Uniseriate. In one row.

Unitunicate. Having a single-layered ascus wall.

Urceolate. Pitcher-like, hollow and contracted at the mouth like an urn.

Uredinales. The rust fungi; obligate plant parasites in the Basidiomycotina.

Urediniospore. A binucleate repeating spore borne in the uredinium. (Uredinales) (Also uredospore, urediospore.)

Uredinium. The sorus that bears urediniospores in the Uredinales (stage II).

Urediospore. See urediniospore.

Uredium. See uredinium.

Uredosorus. See uredinium.

Uredospore. See urediniospore.

Ustilaginales. The smut fungi; plant parasites in the Basidiomycotina.

V

Vagina. In nematodes: A canal, lined with cuticle, that connects the uterus or uteri with the female gonospore.

Valid. Of taxonomic names and epithets: Published in accordance with several articles of the Code of Nomenclature; such names may be legitimate or illegitimate.

Valve. In nematodes: A structure that regulates the rate and/or direction of intake of materials (e.g., the esophago-intestinal valve or cardia).

Valvulated. Having small valves.

Variety. In fungi: A rank below subspecies. In bacteria: Formerly a rank equivalent to subspecies; currently an infrasubspecific rank which has no official standing in nomenclature.

Vas deferens. In nematodes: A slender, tube-like gonoduct in the male; unites posteriorly with the rectum to form the cloaca.

Vector. An living agent that transmits a pathogen from an infected plant to an uninfected one.

Vegetative reproduction. Asexual reproduction.

Vegetative. A cell or structure that is not producing reproductive structures, usually in the assimilative state.

Vein banding. A symptom of virus-infected leaves in which tissues along the veins are darker green than other laminar tissue.

Vein clearing. A symptom of virus-infected leaves in which veinal tissue is lighter green than that of healthy plants.

Ventral. Front, or lower surface.

Vermicular. Worm-shaped, thickened and bent in places. (Also vermiculate.)

Vermiculate. See vermicular.

Vermiform. Worm-like.

Verrucose. Having small, rounded processes or "warts".

Vertical resistance. In a given cultivar: the existence of differential levels of resistance to different races of a given pathogen.

Vesicle. A bladder-like sac or an evanescent bubble within which zoospores mature; any bubble-like cell or bubble-like membranous structure within a cell.

Vessel. A xylem element or series of such elements whose function is to conduct water and mineral nutrients.

Vestigial. Pertaining to structures or organs that were well developed in an organism's ancestors but have become rudimentary during the course of evolution.

Viable. Living, able to germinate or grow.

Virescence. Greening of tissue that is normally devoid of chlorophyll; the abnormal development of flowers in which all organs are green and partly or wholly transformed into structures like small leaves.

Virescent. A normally white or colored tissue that develops chloroplasts and becomes green.

Virion. The infectious unit of a virus.

Viroid. Any of numerous kinds of small particles (250-400 nucleotides) of circular, single-stranded RNA that is unencapsidated and encodes no known proteins.

Virulence. The degree of pathogenicity of a given pathogen.

Virulent. Capable of causing a severe disease; strongly pathogenic.

Viruliferous. Used to describe a vector containing a virus and capable of transmitting it.

Virus. Infectious units comprising either RNA or DNA enclosed in a protective coat.

Viviparous. Bearing living young.

Volva. A cup-like structure at the base of a basidiocarp (in the Basidiomycetes).

Volvate. Having a volva.

Vulva. In nematodes: Exterior opening of the mature female's reproductive system (female gonopore); generally appears as a transverse slit on the ventral portion of the nematode.

W

Western blot. A protein blot. This term originated as lab jargon; not a generally accepted term.

Wild type. The phenotype characteristic of the majority of individuals of a species under natural conditions.

Wilt. A disease (or symptom) characterized by a loss of turgidity in a plant (e.g., vascular wilt).

Wilting. Of plant disease: A symptom characterized by loss of turgor, which results in drooping of leaves, stems, and flowers.

Witches' broom. An abnormal form of plant growth, most common in woody plants, in which there is a profuse outgrowth of lateral buds to give a "witches' broom" appearance. The shoots may be thickened and may bear abnormal leaves.

Woronin body. A rounded organelle occurring near septa in at least some ascomycetes or deuteromycetes.

Xylem. A plant tissue consisting of tracheids, vessels, parenchyma cells, and fibers; functions in conduction of water and minerals and in structural support of the plant.

Y

Yeast. A unicellular member of the Endomycetales; sometimes used for a non-motile unicellular stage (e.g., of dimorphic animal parasites).

Yellowing. A symptom characterized by the turning yellow of plant tissues that were once green.

Yellows. Any of a wide variety of plant diseases in which a major symptom is a uniform or non-uniform yellowing of leaves and/or other plant components. Yellows may be caused by fungi (e.g., celery yellows), viruses (e.g., sugar beet yellows virus), bacteria (e.g., coconut lethal yellowing), protozoa (e.g., hartrot), spiroplasmas or phytoplasmas.

Z

Zoosporangium. A sporangium within which zoospores are produced.

Zoospore. An asexual, motile spore that bears one or two flagella.

Zygomycotina. A subdivision of fungi characterized by the formation of a thick-walled resting spore formed after the fusion of two equal gametangia.

Zygosporangium. In the Zygomycotina: A usually thick-walled, often ornamented, multinucleate resting sporangium formed following anastomosis of gametangia arising from compatible mycelia (in heterothallic species) or from the same mycelium (in homothallic species).

Zygospore. A sexual resting spore formed within a zygosporangium.

Zygote. A diploid cell resulting from the union of two gametes; a diploid nucleus resulting from the union of two haploid nuclei.